'*The Art of Mindful Baking* is a sweet fruit of
Julia Ponsonby's 25 years of cooking and baking at
Schumacher College. This beautifully written book will
inspire the reader to take up baking as a delightful
activity and spiritual practice. This book will lead
you to mindful living.'

SATISH KUMAR
EDITOR-IN-CHIEF OF *RESURGENCE & ECOLOGIST*

'Julia Ponsonby reminds us with gentle eloquence that
to achieve the simplicity that defines good baking and cooking
requires attention to the ingredients, consciousness of the
processes and awareness of all the collaborators involved – not
least ourselves. There's a serenity about this book that bodes
well for every kitchen in which it is used.'

ANDREW WHITLEY
AUTHOR OF *BREAD MATTERS* &
CO-FOUNDER OF THE REAL BREAD CAMPAIGN

Mindfulness *in* Baking

Meditations on Bakes & Calm

Julia Ponsonby

Leaping Hare Press

Quarto

First published in the UK in 2014.

This hardback edition first published in 2023 by Leaping Hare Press,
an imprint of The Quarto Group.
One Triptych Place
London, SE1 9SH
United Kingdom
T (0)20 7700 6700
www.Quarto.com

A catalogue record for this book is available from the British Library.

ISBN 978-0-7112-8823-2
Ebook ISBN 978-0-7112-8824-9
Audiobook ISBN 978-0-7112-8873-7

10 9 8 7 6 5 4 3 2 1

Design by Ginny Zeal

Printed in China

CONTENTS

THE AGE-OLD ART OF THE HEARTH

*Watching the flames of an open fire flickering
blue, orange, red, golden, it is as if these warming
feather-flames are telling us a story – but it is almost
impossible to catch the threads and follow it. The story
of bread-making is a bit like that. At one extreme, it
connects us with life at its most basic, elemental and
sustaining – at another, with technological innovation,
social change and justice. Bread is just one aspect of
baking, but it is the cornerstone: the baker's art; the
tempter when warm, the staple when cool. In this book
we will first tell its story, giving it a context for
yesterday, today and tomorrow; then we will
dance with our dough and meet its cousins.*

BAKING IN CHILDHOOD

◆

As a small child I was introduced to the art of cake-baking by our family cleaner, Doris Tovey. She asked only that we grease the tins, watch her cream the butter and sugar — and, best of all, lick out the bowl. As our small arms grew stronger, we were allowed to do more stirring and to know a little more about what was going on, but not much more!

WE KNEW THAT BAKING POWDER made the cake rise and that you needed certain ingredients — butter, sugar, eggs, flour and milk (in that order) — to make a delicious Victoria sandwich. We also knew that both spongy layers must be sandwiched together with jam, ready for serving up at teatime, adorned with a snowy dusting of icing sugar. Because we had no responsibility for making the cake perfect or ready on time, cake-baking with Doris was pure unadulterated fun. We watched, we listened, we got stuck in — we were completely attentive to the goal of baking.

Though we didn't realize it at the time, we were stunning examples of 'mindfulness' in action. For nothing occupied our minds but the delicious cake we were baking. We were engaging as *beginners* — our minds fresh, open to the possibilities of that moment. It is this 'beginner's mind' that many adults set out to cultivate when they consciously introduce a mindful approach to their lives.

Mindfulness in the Mix

The practice of mindfulness is one that has spread across Europe and America in recent years, partly through the teachings of the Vietnamese monk Thich Nhat Hanh.

To be mindful is to centre our awareness in the present moment; it is to be aware of the here and now, second by second. Thoughts of the past and future may appear; we simply acknowledge them and move our focus back to the present. In keeping our awareness open, we look at life with new eyes.

Though the roots of mindfulness meditation can be found in Buddhism, the value of mindfulness practice has been found to have benefits that go far beyond a religious life; it encourages relaxation, and its success in mainstream healthcare, including for the treatment of depression among other ailments, is increasingly well recognized. Because of the slowing down that mindfulness encourages, it has come to be seen as the antidote to our fast-paced modern lives.

Breath as a Bridge

Mindfulness can be described as having a formal and an informal aspect. The formal aspect takes the shape of meditation; the informal aspect resides in applying mindfulness to all we do. In both cases awareness of our own breath – *in … and out … in … and out* – is what anchors our experience respectfully in the present, for breath is always in the present. In his

'Breath is the bridge which connects life to
consciousness, which unites your body to your thoughts.
Whenever your mind becomes scattered, use your breath as
the means to take hold of your mind again.'

FROM 'THE MIRACLE OF MINDFULNESS' BY THICH NHAT HANH
BEACON PRESS, 1987

---

book *The Power of Now,* Eckhart Tolle advocates breath as a
means of centring ourselves in our bodies and of reconnect-
ing with the real world – something that is evermore
important as we often find this connection compromised by
fast-paced modern living.

Mindful Baking

Successful baking requires us to be mindful. It needs us to be
fully present with our activity, engaged in a flow that is imper-
vious to distractions. It asks us to approach recipes with a
'beginner's mind' – not assuming that everything will always
go according to plan. This is the best plan when it comes to
any kind of cooking (or, indeed, living). You may be baking
in a different kitchen with a new oven, and the cooking times
will be different. Even changes in air temperature and humid-
ity can affect the way in which bread dough rises from one
day to the next. And there is always the possibility that a stray
dog might break into your larder and wolf down half the

ingredients so that your meal plans have to change! With a 'beginner's mind' approach, such fluctuations are more a source of surprise than of annoyance – and annoyance is a seasoning that you don't want to let into your baking.

Tapping into Childhood Experiences

As the Head of Food at Schumacher College in Devon, and one of the College's main bakers, I use my 'beginner's mind' approach when my work doesn't go to plan. And I never forget memories of baking cakes with Doris, even though I am now 'playing' on a much larger scale, producing more bread than cake – and doing a lot of organizing as well. Part of the joy of working at a place that is a centre for transformative education for sustainable living is that wonderful, open-minded people from all over the world arrive on our doorstep. They join us in the kitchen, bringing freshness to all that we prepare. The eagerness to learn, and give, that flows from our participants is infectious and takes me back time and again to my childhood baking experiences. Amid the rush to get meals out on time, I find myself looking at things with new eyes and seeing new possibilities in familiar recipes. Cooking together becomes a bit like 'jamming', to use a musical term. It's an opportunity to be creative together, to share ideas. This element of play is something that we can all bring to our baking; it is an often-forgotten aspect of the meditative approach that brings revitalization and joy.

Playing with Fire

Long ago, at the dawn of our written history, a great weight of importance was placed on the shoulders of Hestia, the ancient Greek goddess of the hearth and home. As a result of a bargain struck with her brother, Zeus, to remain a free woman, Hestia looked after the cooking for him, keeping the sacred fire at the centre of Mount Olympus burning. This made her accountable for nurture – and underlined the age-old link between the art of the hearth and well-being.

TODAY IT IS STILL THE ARCHETYPAL WARMTH represented by Hestia's hearth that draws us close when we are hungry, cold or even bored. It is the skilful use of this hearth that enables us to take nature's offerings and transform them into baked goods, which are perhaps the most tempting of all the foods that we have the pleasure to eat. When we bake with our modern ovens we are in essence using the same primordial fire of old, and it requires respect, skill and mindfulness about what we are making.

The History of Baking

Humans and baking go back a long way. As long as 23,000 years ago evidence shows that humans were processing and consuming wild cereal grains. By the Neolithic period in 9500 BCE people were using simple stone tools to smash and

'In preparing anything one does not only put
one's magnetism into it, but the voice of one's soul is
produced in the thing one prepares . . . If the cook is
irritated while cooking, if she is grumbling, if she
is sighing, if she is miserable, wretched, all that
comes before you with the food she prepares. It is the
knowledge of this fact which made the Hindus engage
as a cook a high-caste Brahmin, whose evolution was
great, whose life was pure, whose thoughts were
elevated . . . who is sometimes the guru, the teacher.'

HAZRAT INAYAT KHAN (1882–1927)
FOUNDER OF THE SUFI ORDER IN THE WEST IN 1914
& TEACHER OF UNIVERSAL SUFISM

grind various cereals to remove the inedible outer husks.
When mixed with water and left to dry in the sun, a porridgey mix made from the interior of the grain would have risen
slightly in the warmth and, with the influence of wild yeasts
in the air (perhaps blown from the surface of nearby fruits),
would have formed a bread-like crust. This early 'rock-bak-
ing' would have been unpredictable, but its product can be
seen as the precursor of the bread we know today.

By the time of the ancient Egyptians, some 4,000 years
ago, the skill of baking was distinctly recognizable and had
begun to be refined with scientific precision, giving status to

those who learned the art of bread-making. The process of taking a piece of fermented dough and saving it, to kick-start the next day's loaf, was discovered, and continues to be the way we make sourdough today (*see page 90*). One of the oldest crafts in the world was born and began to spread to all parts of Europe, including Greece and the Roman Empire.

Campaigns for Bread

However, the history of baking has been punctuated by periods when the quality of our daily bread dropped dangerously, and intervention and campaigning were required to bring it back up to scratch. For example, in the thirteenth century, the Assize of Bread and Ale brought in a long-lasting weight regulation that prevented bakers from pinching from the loaves they sold. This triggered a more serious attitude towards the quality of bread, its baking and selling – so much so that baking apprenticeships often lasted several years. To show their responsibility, bakers frequently threw in an extra loaf to demonstrate that they were not cheating – hence the expression 'a baker's dozen', meaning 13, not 12.

Later, at the time of the Industrial Revolution, the threat to bread quality returned. First, because the prairies of North America were opened up, providing huge wheat fields for the burgeoning population of Britain; and, second, because the invention of a roller-milling system meant that for the first time whiter flour and bread could be produced for everyone.

Now came the dangers that bread might be whitened artificially with the toxic chemical known as alum – and that the nutritional value of the minerals and vitamins present in the wholewheat germ might be lost. A decline in public health in late-Victorian and early twentieth-century England was linked to a decline in the quality of the staple loaf, and so a campaign began for a standard loaf. So much was the value of brown bread re-appreciated, that during the Second World War, white bread was banned for eight years.

Today, with reality-TV baking competitions reviving interest in home baking around the world, it looks as if the nurturing fires at the heart of our homes are being tended once again. However, as any Scout will know, it is not the blaze of the fire that counts, but the sustained and regular feeding with appropriate logs and sticks, the gentle blowing and nurturing. It is this that we need to sustain as we move into a post-petroleum era, where survival skills are once again more deeply rooted in community life and appreciated for the way they knit our lives together.

The Demise of Bread

Sadly, the 'holistic' aspect of the 'good' bread lesson was not entirely learned in the post-war years, and we are once again at a punctuation point in the history of bread-making. The latest story began in 1961, as new technology seemed to herald an era of better bread. That year the Chorleywood

Baking Process (CBP) was introduced and soon spread throughout the bread-eating world, sending traditional sourdough methods into decline.

Basically, by adding more yeast, vegetable fat and 'improvers', and by throwing in an intensive high-speed mix and a vigorous shaking, the bread-making process was reduced to three-and-a-half hours and came to involve no fermentation period at all. More than 50 years since the inception of the CBP, about 80 per cent of UK bread is still made using this speeded-up process. This nutritionally-empty white bread now accounts for 50 per cent of what we buy, and yet overall bread consumption has halved since 1960.

All the positive benefits that went into the traditional slow process have been lost. As Andrew Whitley, in his book *Bread Matters* explains: 'fermenting doughs for 6 hours as opposed to 30 minutes removes around 80 per cent of a potentially carcinogenic substance called acrylamide that is found in bread crusts, and long yeast fermentations conserve the highest levels of B vitamins in dough (48 per cent of vitamin B1 is lost in rapidly made white bread).'

Over the past decade, articles in peer-reviewed journals of nutrition and medicine have shown that eating bread with longer fermentation periods, of up to 24 hours, has many other benefits, including a lower Glycaemic Index. This leaven bread is more digestible and results in fewer symptoms of bloating, stomach upsets and cramps – even when compared to bread made with the same flour, but using the CBP. This could be because the lactic-acid bacteria in sourdough help to 'pre-digest' wheat and rye flour, making it less allergenic.

The Revival of Artisan Bread-Making

The good news is that the sorry state of commercial bread is being matched by the development of artisan bakeries and bakery schools throughout Britain and by a rise in home-baking, often tutored by articulate, high-profile sourdough teachers, such as Andrew Whitley and Dan Lepard.

In America, a revival of the artisan bread-making movement has been steadily gathering pace for the last 30 years, with bakers such as Steve Sullivan, Daniel Leader and Jim Lahey at its helm. In an article in *The Monthly* entitled 'Upper Crust', Andrea Pflaumer traces this renaissance to the Tassajara Zen Centre.[1] This strikes a chord with me, as one of my first attempts at making sourdough was using a recipe from the *Tassajara Bread Book*, presented to me by its author, Edward Espe Brown, on a teaching trip to Schumacher College. Ed was one of a group of Zen Buddhist monks who began baking as a form of meditation. Soon local mills were opening in the San Francisco Bay area to feed the local home-bakers, and new artisan bakeries began to start up. Today San Francisco has been reinstated as the sourdough capital of America (a reputation it gathered as long ago as 1847). Mass-production factory technology is slowly being undermined.

---

[1] 'Upper Crust' by Andrea Pflaumer, *The Monthly*, v.37, n.2, 1 November 2006 (accessed on www.mindfully.org, April 2014)

Pain Poilâne

The revival of artisan bread has taken its inspiration from the European tradition of sourdough breads, including the dark rye breads of Germany, the crusty white baguettes of France and the olive-encrusted focaccias of Italy, to name but a few. However, one bread stands out as a major catalyst in the revival of the sourdough tradition: the large, round, 85 per cent wholewheat pain Poilâne, or 'miche' bread, from the Paris bakeries of the Poilâne family. Back in 1932, Pierre Poilâne believed strongly in the importance of a hands-on approach to baking, and in the use of stone-ground flour, natural fermentation and wood-fired ovens. When his son Lionel took over the bakery in the Seventies he continued this tradition, but introduced a 'retro-innovation' in the form of machine-kneading. Today, pain Poilâne is produced both for local consumption and for export worldwide, with 15,000 loaves per day being produced from 24 wood-fired ovens at the bakery's Bièvres facility in Paris.

In Australia, too, artisan bakeries are on the rise and people are buying sourdough. And there are advocates such as Warwick Quinton who bake, build ovens and teach. Production (it would seem) is currently lagging behind demand, because in 2013, supermarkets were found to be souring their regular yeasted bread with citric acid, to pass it off as artisan bread. This spurred a nationwide demand for the kind of definition of real bread that the UK's Real Bread Campaign has also been arguing for. Put simply: flour, salt, water and yeast; *no* undeclared additives.

The Role of Fast Food

Through his writing and public talks, author of *The Omnivore's Dilemma* Michael Pollan reveals that bread is not the only victim of the fast-food industry. Instead, what has happened with mainstream bread production may be seen as symptomatic of a broader cultural move that links the fast-food movement with the return of women to the workplace after the Second World War. Pollan describes how in the 'post-Betty Friedan' America of the Sixties it was advertising that drew women towards fast food, by presenting ready meals as a means of combining the role of food-provider with career woman, for whom there appeared to be no time to cook from scratch. In the process, women risked losing a part of their traditional role that they had rated as creative and relaxing: cooking. The care of the hearth began to be contracted out.

Can 'Fast Food' Feed Body & Spirit?

Today most people buy their bread and all their baked goods. These basic staples have become passengers in the fast-food lane. But what is 'fast food'? Usually the term refers to food that has been produced in an energy-intensive way outside the home. On arrival, its consumer may add a few finishing touches – tempting the idea that this is still 'home-cooking'.

Unfortunately, this convenience food comes at a cost: it is usually laden with hidden salts, sugars and preservatives, and its sudden arrival on our dinner table divorces us from the connective process that is involved in food creation. It therefore deprives us of a wholeness-affirming activity, in much the same way as an over-dependence on motorized transport deprives us of exercise that is vital to our physical well-being. Baking does not lend itself to being fast – it lends itself to being slow – and baked goods lend themselves to being shared, and to being kept.

In his book *Cooked: A Natural History of Transformation,* Michael Pollan reports that home-cooking in the usa has declined by 50 per cent from what it was in the mid-Sixties, with a daily average of just 27 minutes being spent on cooking, and four minutes on cleaning up. And there appears to be a direct correlation between the abandonment of cooking and the increase in levels of obesity, because when you let industry cook for you, all the unhealthy hidden fats, sugars, salts and additives start creeping into your daily food. 'Special occasion food becomes everyday food', and this does not make for a healthy habit! The moral is that home-cooking deserves to be revalued: it's a spontaneously *mindful* activity, all the more so for being very simple most of the time.

Slow Food is Soul Food

On cue to counter the fast-food business is the Slow Food movement, which has now been gathering force for more than 20 years. Like mindfulness, this movement puts quality before quantity, and advocates slowing down the pace of life so that there is time to really appreciate the 'taste' of each moment. The birth of Slow Food was triggered in 1986, when McDonald's threatened to open a fast-food restaurant at the bottom of the Spanish Steps in Rome. The Slow Food movement's founder, Carlo Petrini, set out to oppose this, declaring, 'This is a battle we will win with our knives and forks.' Slow Food champions the centrality of the dinner table and families eating together, as opposed to the TV-meals syndrome, a more antisocial pattern of eating that has been fed by the fast-food industry's microwave meals and takeaways.

Slow Food groups known as 'convivia' have now spread throughout the world. Regular international meetings are convened in Italy to share tastings, and the Salone del Gusto in Turin is the world's largest food-and-wine fair, with old varieties of food being cooked, sold and shared. And, though the Slow movement has mushroomed beyond food to other areas of life (Slow Cities, Slow Gardening and so on) food is still at its core. With Slow Food Kids, the movement is trying to give youngsters a richer perspective on food, and enable them to appreciate its real quality via all five senses: smelling it, touching it, tasting it, looking at it, and even listening to it.

Tuning into Mindfulness in the Kitchen

A volunteer from the Findhorn Foundation recently joined us to help cook lunch at the College. During our time together, she described to me how each of their cooking sessions in this spiritual and ecological learning community began with a few moments of 'attunement', when feelings were shared and a positive framework was created. Many years ago I used to start all my cooking sessions in a similar way, bringing all the cooks together for a moment of centring and focusing. Nowadays we are cooking for so many people, and with so many diverse groups, that it has become rather difficult to get our starting times coordinated. However, once people get stuck into their particular task, they are mindful and our kitchen is always a happy place to be. The joy of working on your own, in contrast to social cooking, is that you can set your own scene – you can choose the music or the silence, or even turn your cooking into a meditation!

Before embarking on any of the recipes in this book, it is worth engaging in a few preparatory moments of breathing, following the simple mindful-breathing exercise opposite. It is inspired by the method for training your breath in the 16-step Buddhist text known as the Sutra of Mindfulness, as originally taught by the Buddha.

MINDFUL-BREATHING EXERCISE

❋

Begin the sequence by 'resetting' your breath as follows:

• Take a deep breath IN and then let it whoosh powerfully OUT . . . Then hold still, with no breathing, for three seconds.

• Breathe IN slowly, feeling your diaphragm stretch down and your lungs and chest stretch out.

• Breathe OUT even more slowly.

• Keep breathing IN and OUT like this for a few minutes, being aware that it is the out-breath that slows everything down.

• Feel the cool air coming through your nostrils on your in-breath, and the tinkling warm air rushing out through your nose on your out-breath, as your chest sinks.

• If you like, say to yourself, 'I am breathing in a long breath', 'I am breathing out a long breath'; OR 'I am breathing in a short breath', 'I am breathing out a short breath'; OR 'I am feeling my whole body through my breath', 'I am feeling my whole breath-body'.

• When thoughts come, do not judge them, or cast them away, or indulge them. Simply return your mind graciously to your breathing. Because it exists in the present moment, following your breath invites you to be in the 'now' too.

RECIPES

CHAPTER ONE

SIMPLICITY

*Like breathing, simplicity has a fundamental
presence that spreads harmony into art, health,
culture — perhaps into all things, because it too is
one of life's great universals. Can we therefore use
simplicity as a kind of 'litmus test' for what is
good and wholesome about food? In the process
we may discover what it is about simplicity
that supports both genuine relationship
and integrity in our baking.*

THE BREAD OF LIFE

◆

When my son was small, our neighbouring farmer would let him slide down the hills of grain in his huge barn without fear of an avalanche. At that time I came the closest I have come in all my baking experience to closing the bread-production loop.

O SCAR EAGERLY FILLED HIS POCKETS and socks with barley and wheat, intended as cattle food, and walked home with his pockets bulging and his socks swinging like javelins. Once home, he would not be put off by any far-too-scientific notions (for a three-year-old) that the wheat in Devon was too low in gluten to produce good bread, due to a lack of sunshine. And so we developed a technique of grinding the grain, first in an old-fashioned manual coffee-grinder, then in an electric coffee-grinder and finally using a sieve to remove excess fibre. We mixed the flour with yeast, salt, water and honey; kneaded it; let it rise; baked it. Warm from the oven and spread with butter, it provided a greedily devoured bedtime snack. No matter that it was dense, this was bread made with the grains Oscar had watched the combine-harvester mow from the field, then toss into lorries that danced alongside it, perfectly synchronized in speed.

For me, this grass-roots journey from grain to bread characterizes the way 'simplicity', by its very nature, offers us a slice of experience that is both direct and satisfying. It makes room for a relationship that understands how things work and where things come from. Unfortunately this is a relationship that has often been sacrificed in the age of supermarkets, convenience cooking and fast food. However, by engaging in simplicity, we can see and feel these connections more clearly – and our eyes are opened.

Exploring Simplicity

Taking the analysis of simplicity one step further, it seems to me that simplicity is, in a sense, a threefold, almost archetypal phenomenon. For example, in relation to baking there are three important aspects to bear in mind. First, there is simplicity of content – in the sense of the ingredients being pure and unadulterated. Second, there is a simplicity of form, which ensures that the physical form of a baked good does not distract from the content, and inspires a response of pleasure in relationship to its look, feel and touch. Third, there is an experiential dimension to everything we bake, because the goal is to eat it – in this case a wholesome and flavourful 'munch' ticks the third box: simplicity of experience.

Food offers a good way to explore this threefold notion of simplicity, because our capacity for taste is so discerning and so direct in its communicative power. Our tongues work closely in tune with three of our other senses: smell, sight and touch. And these senses contribute to, and often trigger, mental associations that we have built up over time.

Honouring Simplicity

Good, wholesome bread offers an excellent example of simplicity. Very few ingredients are required to bake a huge variety of breads; add a few more ingredients (eggs, sugar, butter) and you can include cakes and biscuits, to give an even wider range of baked goods. But bread is typically the simplest and most basic.

Throughout the world, wheat, water, salt and a leaven are combined and worked in subtly different ways to achieve a rich assortment of breads, including French baguettes, braided challahs, pocketed pittas, skinny pretzels and ringed bagels, to name but a few. Grains with a flavour and gluten content unique to a particular place feed into the association of particular breads with particular peoples and places. But although each loaf has been uniquely shaped by its culture, all breads are recognizable as belonging to the same global family of staple nutrition. They are the starch-bringers, in wheaten form. In everything we bake, let us honour this fundamental threefold simplicity and not overlook or disguise it, so that the joy of simplicity in all its aspects is still there when our creations emerge from the oven.

Generating Food-Trust

This is particularly important today. Sometimes in the modern world simplicity of content gets lost, in an attempt to re-create an old favourite at a cheaper cost. For example, we may love white bread – crusty on the outside, and spongy with butter-welcoming holes on the inside – but does this mean that white bread made by the Chorleywood Baking Process (*see page 15*) is an embodiment of true simplicity? Would we want the result if we knew that this bread would not ultimately deliver – in terms of satisfaction or nutrition – because its contents were far from the simple substances suggested by its form?

When you add artificial ingredients, you may be taken on a journey of craving that is difficult to satisfy. For example, my grandmother loved a little sweetness in her tea – but she didn't want to have the calories that come with sugar, so she used saccharin tablets instead. She began by taking two tablets, but soon she was adding six tablets to each cup – because the false sweetness wasn't satisfying, she craved more and more. When you bake your own bread you are the creator of simple food that will meet your body's needs and give you confidence in what you eat. This food-trust will aid your digestion, because you will be more relaxed when you eat.

Simplicity of Process
It is tempting to add another dimension to this concept of simplicity: *simplicity of process*. In this fourth dimension I would include a baking routine that is, as far as possible, carried out *without* dependence on industrial tools or equipment. The baking process is not visible in the finished product, but

it *is* implicit in it. However, because some of the processes for making traditional breads worldwide involve varying degrees of manipulation and resting that are quite complex (though they become routine for people who use them regularly), it seems better to stick with a concept of simplicity that focuses on the product. Nonetheless, if you are tempted to make bread in a bread machine, bear in mind that you will not have that same connection with the simplicity of process that is so satisfying when you make a loaf of bread by hand.

To experience simplicity through baking, try making the following wholesome, single-rise loaf of spelt bread, which doesn't require any kneading. Use the step-by-step process as a vehicle to focus your thoughts, while at the same time allowing your hands, your ingredients and also your oven to engage in manifesting an embodiment of simplicity.

You could make the process even simpler by using your own natural leaven or starter (*see page 90*), but as getting a natural starter ready takes a few days, the shortcut of using fresh or dried yeast makes for a convenient starting point, especially if you are a baking beginner. Likewise, milling your own grains would connect you more firmly with the initial stages of the whole process and would bring health benefits too (*see page 50*), but a bag of organic flour from a wholefood shop is almost as good. Fresh baker's yeast is normally available from bakeries where bread is being made on the premises, though you may have to ask for it.

SIMPLE SPELT BREAD

Spelt is the ancient form of wheat that was used by the Romans. Because it has not been hybridized, like the rest of our modern wheat, many people with wheat allergies find they can eat spelt without any negative effects. However, spelt does contain gluten, so it should not be eaten by true coeliacs, who experience an unpleasant autoimmune response to gluten, in whatever shape or form it occurs.

The most successful spelt bread results when the flour is mixed into a very moist dough, using either yeast (as below) or a sourdough method (see page 92).When this consistency is achieved, the dough rises well and produces a spongy wholewheat loaf that is full of flavour and high in fibre – as well as being moist and well aerated. Such is the sweet, earthy, nutty taste of pure wheat – I love it.

Makes *1 loaf (12–14 slices)*

Preparation time 15 minutes, plus 45–65 minutes rising

Baking time about 45–50 minutes

Special equipment 1-kg/2-lb loaf tin, oiled, and dusted with a little spelt flour

Ingredients

• Sunflower oil, for oiling • 300 ml/10 fl oz warm water
• 1 tsp dried yeast or 10 g/¼ oz fresh yeast, crumbled • 1 tsp honey (optional) • 400 g/14 oz spelt flour, plus extra for dusting • 3 tbsp sunflower seeds (optional) • 1 tsp salt
• Beaten egg or milk or soya milk for brushing (optional)

Method

1. Measure the warm water into a jug. It should be lukewarm, blood temperature – baby's bathwater – 37°C/98°F. Some people like to get this temperature by combining one quarter boiling water with three quarters cold. *As you touch the water with your fingers they will feel happy with the warmth. This is your cue for remembering: here is the temperature of warm-blooded life. The fact it feels pleasant to me connects me with the majority of other life around me, not just mammals but associated bacteria and fungi.*

2. Stir in the yeast and honey, *remembering that the bees who made it took a lifetime just to collect one-twelfth of a teaspoon.* Leave to froth or, with the fresh yeast, stir it in until dissolved. If you are using fast-acting (super-fine) yeast, stir this into the flour. I like using fresh yeast or traditional dried yeast because I like watching it bubble up and feel reassured by seeing it come alive. *When you look at the yeast coming alive, remember this single-celled fungus is part of the incredible kingdom of fungi that create an underground web of tubes connecting the roots of plants in ecosystems and distributing nutrients and information between them.*

3. In a large bowl, combine the flour, 2 tablespoons sunflower seeds, if using, and salt. Make a well in the middle and pour in the yeasty water. Mix until you have a soft dough that is sticky to touch, but not runny or lumpy.

4. Either scoop the dough straight into the prepared loaf tin and press gently into shape with damp hands, OR knead/roll it lightly on a floured surface to shape. It is not necessary to knead the dough, you are just giving it a smooth shape by pressing its surface into a little extra flour – this will only take a minute, then place the loaf into the tin, half filling it. Either brush with egg or milk and sprinkle with the remaining sunflower seeds, or spray/splash the top with water.

5. Leave the loaf to rise in a warm place for 45–65 minutes, or until doubled in size: the time this takes will depend largely on the ambient temperature and will vary with the season and weather. *To tune into what is going on within the loaf, go away then come back after 20 minutes and stand in front of the bread observing it closely. Can you notice that the dough is gradually swelling up and filling the tin? Imagine the yeast feeding off the sugars in the starch and giving off carbon dioxide, which in turn creates bubbles that are held in place by the glutinous structure of the wheat, a bit like blowing a bubble in bubble gum. Perhaps, when it's time to put the bread in the oven, you'll hear the slightest crackle of popping as some of these bubbles reach the surface and burst.*

6. Preheat your oven to 180°C/350°F/Gas Mark 4.

7. When ready, the bread will have completely filled the bread tin and the centre may be poking out above the edge by 1–2 cm/½ –¾ inches. Bake on the middle shelf for about 45 minutes, or until it sounds hollow and drum-like when tapped on the base. Cool on a wire rack. Before the bread is cold, tempt yourself with the first crusty slice, spread with butter. Don't cut a second slice, as without the structural support of the 'heel', your loaf will easily be squashed or misshapen.

Now isn't that a simple pleasure? For me, it is – both in terms of baking and of eating – and I will make this basic bread over and over again. When I have no urgency to produce my next loaf in a hurry, I sometimes choose to bake this bread using *half* the amount of yeast. This doubles the rising time, but gives the flavours (and the healthful lactic acid) longer to develop, so it's a good exercise. When it's convenient, try leaving your bread to rise slowly in the fridge overnight, too!

INFORMED BAKING

In an age when we can no longer be confident about our ingredients, the dimension of mindfulness that brings clarity to a situation is critically important for the conscientious baker. Seeing clearly is the goal of active, 'analytic' meditation – and of every honest Fair Trade or ethical supplier who offers products on the open market, and of every ethical review body.

THE STARTING PREMISE is that we need to know our ingredients – where they come from and what the environmental cost of producing them has been. If we are mindful, our baking will depend upon us being satisfied that we have sourced our ingredients with integrity. We must establish a bottom line, and only cook when this has been met.

Nowadays there are various ethical and organic websites that you can use to check out the credentials of ingredients –

and through which you can contact producers directly. Symbols are used on most packaging to indicate whether ingredients are fairly traded or organic, and *most* ingredients include a note on where they come from, so that you can work out the food miles you are totting up when you cook.

If you buy locally, it's easier to follow the journey of the ingredients in a product; you can even go and visit the farm or factory where they came from. However, the reality is not always that simple. If I were to follow the journey-into-being of one of our own College-made loaves of organic bread last year, our journey would begin in Kazakhstan, due to the poor wheat harvests in the UK during 2012. As an (unintended) antidote to this surprising state of affairs, this year's sustainable-horticulture students have planted their own wheat in the College gardens, with ancient-grain expert and teacher John Letts, so we will be able to participate in the whole process.

Consumption Statistics

It has been estimated that an average of 297 square metres/ 3,200 square feet would be required for a family of four to grow their own wheat to meet their bread needs for a year[1] – that's more personal outdoor space than most people have access to. Nonetheless, there is great value in gaining insight into one of our staple foods. Following the process by doing it yourself is one way of achieving this, even if you only have enough space to produce one loaf of bread. It also helps us

---

[1] 'World warned on food price spiral' by Finlo Rohrer, *BBC News Magazine*, 10 March 2008 (accessed on http://news.bbc.co.uk/1/hi/magazine/7284011.stm, June 2014)

appreciate why wheat-growing and milling have become a specialist activity – it is not such a simple business as growing, say, potatoes. With four million tonnes of flour being made from five million tonnes of wheat every year in the UK, and 12 million loaves being sold each day,[1] it is not surprising that the vast majority of loaves are produced by an automated process. According to the Bakers' Federation review of the European bread market, this could be up to 80 per cent, with only 7 per cent currently produced by craft bakeries. This compares with 66 per cent of sales attributed to packaged/industrial bread in the USA and 33 per cent being accounted for by artisanal or unpackaged bread. However, us consumption of loaf bread is less overall (24 kg/53 lb) per person per year, compared with 50 kg/110 lb per year in the UK and Ireland; 53 kg/117 lb in Australia; and up to 80 kg/176 lb in Austria and Germany. This doesn't mean that overall bread-dough consumption is less per capita in the USA, because much of the American wheat consumption comes in the form of pizza!

The Human Touch
Whether its eventual destiny takes the shape of simple loaves, bagels or pizza, the grain is delivered from farms into the huge, towering steel silos that form a key part of a modern industrial mill. Later, after the flour has been milled, it is sent to a bakery and prepared in 250 kg/550 lb mixers, then (as dough) it is baked in giant ovens, which can be up to

---

[1] Data from the National Association of Master Bakers, quoted in the 'Facts and Figures' section of the Real Bread Campaign website.

39 m/43 yards long. Now bread, it is cooled, wrapped and packed – all without being touched by human hand. When we remove a slice to put in the toaster, ours will be the first hand that this metamorphosed wheat has ever touched.

Contrast this with the situation in days of old, when the grain would have been sown by hand in 'broadcasting' style, harvested by hand with scythe or sickle, threshed by hand, winnowed by hand – and, of course, kneaded by hand. Anyone who wants to grow their own wheat on an allotment, or let it take over their front lawn, can return to this time-honoured way of doing things. Plenty of self-help videos and information are available online; just watching some of this footage gives you a real feeling for the journey of our daily bread.

YOUR SENSORY GUIDE

Touch, smell, sight, taste and sound – our five senses – are the private tools that work for us, guiding us when we bake, and literally making 'sense' of our quest for simplicity. Being able to trust your own senses is far better than relying on thermometers or photographs, or continually asking other people.

I N ALL THE RECIPES IN THIS BOOK there is an invitation to fine-tune the judgement of your senses until you know you can trust them. To begin with, feel the warmth of the water to check it is comfortable, blood-heat, temperature. Smell the yeast as it rises, and later on smell the aroma of bread baking. As you knead, feel the dough becoming smooth and elastic. Sound comes into the equation, too: tap the base of the bread and listen for a hollow sound, which – together with the sight of the bread – tells you it is ready. In baking, all these senses are put to work in everything you make – and as soon as you begin to ignore their messages, you risk your success.

Flexibility

Seasonal cooking is a vehicle for expressing the need for flexibility in life. This provides another opportunity for us to practise operating from a 'beginner's mind' standpoint.

Eating is something we need to do every day – or almost every day. We can't always wait to have the exact ingredients for a recipe to hand. Indeed, the foundation for the provision of our daily food comes from knowing how to cook temptingly with what is available in our garden and our store cupboard, and *not* in knowing how to follow a recipe that involves specific (and possibly unseasonal or expensive) ingredients. The practice comes first; the recipes second. Being able to use a recipe as a guideline to mindfully create a seasonal dish is vitally important – and it doesn't need to be a recipe that is written down. It could be a hand-me-down recipe taught to you by your grandmother, or a 'felt' recipe that comes to life in your mind's eye as you contemplate the ingredients that are available and how they will work together.

Seasonal & Local Produce

The following recipe for a seasonal vegetable bake invites you to substitute different vegetables, depending on the season, and is a plea not to get stuck in the groove of thinking that you must always get hold of one particular ingredient, because you liked the way it tasted in the same dish two months ago. With the aid of modern air travel, you *can* let your ingredients travel around the world for you, but the real culinary delight comes from cooking with what is seasonal and local to where you live – research suggests this usually gives rise to the menu that will be best for you at any one point, offering you the nutrients you need at different times of the year.

Fruit and vegetables that have been forced to grow out of season or travel across the world have often been treated with pesticides, waxes and preservatives, to make them look fresher. However, they lack antioxidants, minerals, vitamins and trace elements that are present in local food harvested in season. Coordinating our diet with the seasons also prevents us overloading our body with the same foods, which can lead to the development of food intolerances. In her book *The Seasonal Detox Diet*, Carrie L'Esperance presents the seasonal diet as one that naturally cleanses the body and is beneficial for the environment. It also reduces the carbon footprint and supports local farmers. (For further references to research in this area, see Christina Luisa's article 'Eating Seasonally – one of your allies', *Natural News*, 15 April 2012.)

SEASONAL VEGETABLE BAKE

One of the keys to success with this recipe is to incorporate a good quantity of root vegetables (carrots, parsnips, swede, beetroot and potato), because they will hold their shape well when cooked. I have also included mushrooms, which tend to be grown all year round in an indoor environment with controlled heating. (At Dartington we have a local grower who grows oyster mushrooms on coffee grounds, and sells kits, so that everyone else can do the same.) If you don't have 'goose-egg'-sized potatoes, other sizes can also be used, though they may be more breakable if larger, or more fiddly if smaller.

Serves *6–8*

Preparation time 30–40 minutes, plus 8 hours soaking

Baking time 30–45 minutes

Special equipment 2-litre/3½-pint ceramic casserole or pie dish, with a good 5–6 cm/2–2½ inches depth

Ingredients

VEGETABLE FILLING

• 140 g/5 oz dried chestnuts (double if using fresh/hydrated)
• 200 g/7 oz squash • 3–5 tbsp olive oil • 2 medium carrots or 150 g/5½ oz swede, parsnip or turnip or use more squash
• 1 medium leek • 1 medium onion • 100 g/3½ oz fennel or 2–3 celery sticks • 150 g/5½ oz chestnut mushrooms
• 1–2 tsp finely chopped fresh rosemary or thyme or use half quantity of dried • 2 tbsp finely chopped fresh flat-leaf parsley

SIMPLICITY

SEASONINGS

• Salt and freshly ground black pepper • 3–4 tbsp red wine or sherry • 2 tbsp plain white flour or cornflour • 4 tbsp cold water, plus 250 ml/9 fl oz (or use the carrot cooking water) • 2–3 tbsp tamari • 1–2 tsp Dijon mustard or ½ tsp English mustard

TOPPING

• 800 g/1 lb 12 oz or 5 medium goose-egg-sized potatoes
• 50–85 g/2–3 oz grated medium Cheddar cheese
• 50 g/2 oz grated smoked Cheddar cheese or use more medium Cheddar • 4 tbsp cornflakes whizzed into crumbs in a (clean) coffee grinder or crushed • 50 g/2 oz finely chopped walnuts or whole sunflower seeds • A good drizzle of olive oil and tamari

Method

1. If using dried chestnuts, soak them in cold water for several hours or overnight. When re-hydrated boil for 30–40 minutes until tender, but not falling apart. If it's the season for bonfires and Christmas carol singing and you're using fresh chestnuts, pierce them with a knife and boil them. When cooked, drain and peel away the woody inner and outer shell.
2. Next, turn to the potatoes for the topping. If they are organic, there is no need to peel them, as much of the nutritional value lies just under the skin. Place them in a saucepan of cold water with a pinch of salt. Bring to the boil and cook

until parboiled and still holding their shape. As soon as a knife will slide through them easily, drain and leave to cool while you prepare the filling.

3. Preheat your oven to 200°C/400°F/Gas Mark 6. Cut the squash into quarters. Deseed then peel off the skin using a small knife or a T-shaped peeler. Cut into 1½-cm/¾-inch chunks and tip on to a baking tray. Drizzle with olive oil, a sprinkling of salt and dried herbs. Spread out on the tray so the chunks are in a single layer then roast in the oven for 20–30 minutes until just tender with perhaps the occasional tinge of brown. Leave the oven on.

4. Cut the carrots (or swede or parsnip) into 1½-cm/¾-inch rounds or chunks, then cook in a pan of salted water until just tender. Drain and reserve the cooking water.

5. Trim the bottom ends of the leeks to remove the roots, then cut off the whole whiter 'log' part (below where the leaves start opening out) and rinse. Chop the 'leek-log' into chunky rounds, the same size as the carrots. Once the carrots have been cooking for 5–10 minutes toss the leek in with them – they will cook much more quickly. Discard any tough or old-looking leaves from the remaining part of the leek, then halve lengthways, rinse well and roughly chop.

6. Onions and fennel are amazing citizens of the vegetable kingdom, who reveal interesting growth patterns that can be observed more easily than with leeks. Having sliced an onion through from tip to root, it is worth stopping to behold these patterns before cutting them into 1½–2-cm/½–¾-inch pieces. *The many concentric layers of an onion that grow outwards from its small button-like stem are in fact leaves that have been adapted for food storage by the plant, which is why they are so moist and fleshy. The bulb is a resting stage enabling the plant to get through arid periods, before it resumes growth ready to send out a single beautiful 'pom-pom like' flower head, that will produce seeds.*

Another famous thing about onions is that preparing them may make us cry! When you slice through the cell walls sulphur compounds escape irritating our lachrymal glands and causing irritation and tears. There are a higher concentration of these at the base of the onion, so peeling back the brown skin and leaving the root intact can help reduce this reaction, (as can chilling the onion before use, chopping under running water or wearing goggles). The following, however, is my preferred technique for handling onions: slice the whole onion in half lengthways through the root before peeling, then pull back the brown skin to form a 'handle' with the root. With the cut surface of the onion lying flat on your chopping board, the root should be the last part of the onion you chop across. Cut the fennel or celery into 1½–2-cm/½–¾-inch pieces.

7. Halve or quarter the mushrooms depending on how big they are. *Once again stop your journey through the recipe with some observations. Mushrooms come from a different realm to the other vegetables in this bake. They are part of the fungi kingdom which includes microorganisms such as yeast and moulds and is as uniquely different from the kingdom of plants as plants are from animals. What* we commonly recognize as a 'mushroom' is in fact the short-lived fruiting body of fungi preparing to release its spores. Even more extraordinary are the activities of fungal organs we don't normally see. Below the surface of a forest soil, vast networks of interconnecting hollow fungal tubes known as mycelia manage the nutrients of the forest by sending sugars produced by trees in sunny areas into the roots of trees living in more shady places, thereby maintaining the diversity of the whole ecosystem.

8. Going back to the recipe, begin sautéeing the chopped onion and fennel in olive oil stirring regularly with a wooden spatula. Add a pinch of salt and dried herbs, if using. After 2 minutes add the mushrooms and the greener leek tops and cook for 1 further minute. Next, add the wine and cook until all the vegetables are soft.

9. Mix the flour and the 4 tablespoons water together until smooth. Combine with the remaining water, tamari and mustard and add this to the vegetables on the hob, stirring while the liquid thickens.

10. Once the various vegetables are cooked, collect them all in the baking dish, along with the fresh herbs. Mix thoroughly, then taste and adjust the seasoning, and add more carrot water if needed – the liquid level in the casserole should come halfway up the vegetables, any more and it will bubble over and create a mess in your oven.

11. You are now ready to fit the roof on the bake! Slice the cooled potatoes lengthways into 5-mm/¼-inch thick ovals.

Slow down and do this with some care to make sure your starchy 'tiles' are evenly cut. Once your tiles are ready, begin to lay them out on top of the bake working in rows and over-lapping the end of one with the top of the next.

12. When the potato roof is complete, sprinkle half the grated cheese over it, then the crushed cornflakes and chopped nuts. Sprinkle over the remaining grated cheese and follow this with a drizzle of olive oil and tamari. This will give a delicious crispy finish to the dish.

13. Now the bake is assembled, cook in the oven for 30–45 minutes. When ready, a tempting cheesy smell will waft from the oven and the top should be beginning to brown. Insert a knife into the centre of the bake to check that all the vegetables are soft and well cooked.

14. If the top reaches browning point before the vegetables are ready, cover it lightly with foil or greased baking parchment and continue to cook until it is ready. This bake is really a meal in itself, but to add a further dimension, serve the bake with cooked or fresh seasonal greens, such as kale or broccoli.

RECIPES

CHAPTER TWO

USING
OUR HANDS

*Our hands are our most immediate tools,
and they work in perfect harmony with our
brains and our emotions to manifest the diverse
possibilities that grow in our imaginations.
It is our hands that bring about the huge
range of human creativity that we witness in
the physical world. Whether it is in the construction
of an awe-inspiring temple or a tiny hut, a dramatic
sculpture or a simple pot, a lavish dinner
or a humble loaf, our hands are there
making the moves.*

THE MAGIC OF HANDS

◆

The hand is a fantastically complex appendage, with each hand containing 29 major and minor bones, 29 major joints, at least 123 named ligaments, 48 nerves and 30 named arteries — all of which work in concert with the muscles to help perform fine motor skills.

NOT SURPRISINGLY, about one quarter of the motor cortex in the human brain is devoted to the muscles in our hands — our thumb alone is controlled by nine individual muscles, which are in turn controlled by all three major hand nerves. We think of some people having greater dexterity than others, applying the phrase 'They are good with their hands' to someone who is adept at making three-dimensional objects: perhaps in the form of carpentry or painting, stitching or potting — even baking. But the truth is that we're all amazing at manipulating things with our hands, especially when we compare humans with four-legged, cloven-hoofed or finned creatures. The reality is that these hands of ours are unique and they define our species. Both literally and metaphorically, they hold a large part of our magic.

Hands as Tools

Recent research in the US, by Professor David Carrier from the University of Utah, suggests that our hands evolved not just for holding Stone Age tools, but by means of natural selection, for forming punching fists. So the way our hand looks, and its strength, is connected with the violence in our evolutionary history. Comparing our hand with another great-ape hand, our palm is shorter and the fingers longer – thus better for forming fists. In modern times our fists can find a peaceable outlet in the punching-down of dough.

Hands are also good for tearing off bread, and for eating – they were our original eating tool. In fact when forks first appeared in eleventh-century Venice, some clergymen were horrified and said, 'God in his wisdom has provided man with natural forks – his fingers. Therefore it is an insult to him to substitute artificial metallic forks for them when eating.' Today some upmarket us restaurants have been encouraging eating with hands; and *Debrett's*, the bible of British etiquette, has issued a ten-point guide to modern dining manners when eating with the hands.

Hand Cleanliness

Even without finger-food, cleanliness is a critical factor when we involve our hands in the process of eating and cooking. More than any other part of our body, our hands find them-selves in the front line for picking up germs – they touch our phones, stroke our pets, grip shopping trolleys and taps, hit computer keyboards. For this reason, follow the common-sense dictum of washing your hands not only just before you eat, but also before you cook – and why not make this a

loving hand-wash meditation. It's not difficult: warm water and soap, combined with the coming together of our hands in the encircling gesture of washing, is enjoyable and easy to indulge in before any cooking project. Just remember to *notice* and *appreciate* your hands as you wash them, in a more conscious way than usual – and don't forget to scrub your nails!

HARMONY

An agreeable combination of chords in music can evoke a real sense of harmony – a bit like bread-and-butter. When baking, our hands act like conductors, mixing up ingredients to achieve harmony of texture and flavour. The key elements in achieving this are, first, respect for the integrity that rests in wholeness; and, second, appreciating the potential for a harmonious synergy that comes when diverse elements are combined.

A S AN EXAMPLE, LET'S LOOK AT THE VALUE of using whole-grains and milling them freshly – as E.F. Schumacher, the author of *Small is Beautiful*, was practised at doing, and as advocated by the German doctor and nutritionist Dr Max Otto Bruker. By milling our own flour on a regular basis, we can keep the balanced nutrition of the wholegrain intact, without any need to remove those parts of the kernel that don't keep well and can go rancid after a mere 14 days. If we use white flour on its own (or brown flour created by

HAND-AWARENESS MEDITATION

❋

• Make yourself comfortable, sitting in a position that supports your legs and back. Take ten deep breaths in and out. When you have let go of your daily worries and feel relaxed, stretch your hands out before you and let your gaze dwell on them, turning then slowly, so that you see alternately your palms and the backs of your hands.

• How long ago did these hands learn to pinch, pull and prod? Notice how your thumbs work as a team with your fingers. Your 'opposable' thumbs give you a grasping/gripping action, by pinching together with your first finger, enabling you to pick up food, fuel and tools. Try picking up a pencil between thumb and forefinger. This is the primordial great-ape grip – it will seem so spontaneous that you think nothing of it, but once upon a time, you probably practised this grip on your mother's finger. And you practised dropping things too.

• Now bring your palms together, as if you were going to pray. Then slide them up and down against each other until they feel warm, and blow gently upon them. Slow down the motion and, when your hands are completely still again, give them a thank-you for all they have done, for you and with you, over many years.

returning the bran to white flour), the bread's shelf life will be improved, but the nutritional benefits that come from using the wholegrain will be reduced. The germ is not only a source of unsaturated fats (which may go rancid), but of vitamin E, minerals, phytochemicals and B vitamins. The bran, by comparison, provides more vitamins, fibre, phyto-chemicals, some protein and minerals (such as magnesium, iron and zinc). The endosperm (from which white flour is made) provides carbohydrate and protein. If we are to reap the maximum benefit from eating wheat, we should ideally respect the potency of the whole and work with this, which means keeping the elements that make up a single grain together, in the same mouthful.

By contrast, there are other foods that benefit from being split – not only to extend their shelf life, but to improve access to their nutritional content. One such is full-cream milk. In a few shakes you can split milk into curds and whey, to make a very simple butter that will adorn your bread deliciously, giving the perfect harmony of fats and carbohy-drates that tastes so good!

We don't all have the luxury of owning our own mill, and most of us have to get by with the flour we buy in shops, which is still pretty nutritious. Also, I must confess that I enjoy using both white and brown flours with their different culinary features – and their potential for creating all sorts of wonderful food harmonies.

LIGHT-BROWN BREAD OR ROLLS

In contrast with the spelt bread described earlier (see page 31), *this brown bread contains lots of gluten, because it is made with a large proportion of white flour. This gives the dough a lot of elasticity, and means that the open texture will be improved by a good knead.*

Gluten is made up of two proteins: gliadin and glutenin. These are found in the endosperm of the fruits of the grass family, along with the starch. Gluten is a valuable protein that is needed to nourish embryonic plants during germination, and it makes up 80 per cent of wheat's protein. When it comes to well-aerated bread, it is the capacity of gluten to absorb water and expand like bubble-gum without bursting, which makes for the development of the kind of light, spongy loaf we love. The open pockets, or bubbles, are formed as the yeasts feed off the sugars derived from the starch in the flour and give off carbon dioxide. When the bread goes into the oven, the gluten protein coagulates, sets and loses its elasticity – but the bread size, shape and structure will remain the same.

When you first start baking it's good to keep things simple. Later, you may wish to experiment with techniques that artisan bakers use. For example, inserting a baker's stone in the oven an hour before baking simulates the heat in a wood-fired oven and increases 'oven-spring' – the amount that bread rises when put in an oven. Another way to enhance this and improve the crust is to put a dish of water in the base of the oven 10 minutes before baking, then leave it there for the first 10 minutes of baking. The steam conducts heat to the rising loaf more quickly, keeping its surface moist as it expands.

Makes *1 round, oval or rectangular loaf or 10 rolls*

Preparation time 15–20 minutes, plus about 2 hours rising

Baking time 45 minutes

Special equipment 1-kg/2¼-lb loaf tin or baking tray, oiled and floured or lined with baking parchment

Ingredients

• 1–2 tbsp olive or sunflower oil, plus extra for oiling

• 300 g/10 oz strong white organic bread flour, plus extra for dusting • 300 ml/10 fl oz warm water • 1 tsp sugar or honey • 1 tsp dried yeast or 10 g/½ oz/2 tsp fresh yeast, crumbled • 150 g/6 oz organic whole wheat flour

• 1–1½ tsp salt • A little beaten egg for brushing (optional)

Method

1. Place the warm water in a measuring jug, then stir in the sugar and yeast. Leave to froth – or, with the fresh yeast, simply stir until dissolved.

2. In a large bowl, combine the flours and salt.

3. Add the yeasty water and oil and mix until you have a soft dough and all the ingredients are evenly distributed. If the dough seems stiff or leathery, add a little more water. You are aiming for a soft, elastic dough that holds its shape: it may be slightly sticky on the surface, but it should not be sloppy. Knead gently on a lightly floured surface or in the bowl for a few minutes until fairly smooth, then return to the bowl to rise. Spray, brush or smooth the top of the dough with a little more water to prevent the surface drying out (or cover the bowl loosely with a lid or tea towel). Leave to rise in a warm place for 1–2 hours until the dough has doubled in size.

4. Tip the risen dough on to a clean and very lightly floured surface and 'knock back', punching out the carbon dioxide. This is your chance to get the gluten working! You'll notice how much smoother, stronger and more elastic the gluten has now become: the dough has, in a sense, been 'self-kneading' during its rise, for with every new burst of carbon dioxide from the yeast into the bubbles, protein and water molecules move about and have another chance to connect and form more gluten, expanding the microscopic lattice of strands.

5. As you knead, stretch and push the dough away from you with your fists, then bring it back together. You will feel the gluten tightening and springing back. Do this for about 3–5 minutes. Then, let your dough rest for a few minutes so the gluten can relax making your dough easier to form into a loaf ready for its final proving. (The proving or rising stage can also be described as 'fermentation' since the by-product of yeast's feeding is both carbon dioxide and alcohol).

6. If you want to make rolls, pull or cut off tangerine-sized portions of dough and roll these under your palm of your hands until they are round and smooth.

7. For a single loaf, shape the dough into a long oval, or round bread. Keep the joints at the bottom and make sure the top

BUTTER-SHAKING MEDITATION
✳

Makes *60 g / 2½ oz, if using double cream*

Time *as long as it takes — 15 minutes if you're keen and strong!*

Equipment *a 300–400 ml / 10–14 fl oz clean jam jar; a sieve*

Ingredients *150 ml / 5 fl oz cream and a pinch of salt for later*

• Butter-making requires fewer steps than bread-making, but much more physical effort over a shorter period. Simply half-fill your jam jar with cream. (The higher the proportion of fat in the cream, the more butter you will produce.) Make sure the lid is tightly screwed on, then shake and shake... A bread-enthusiast friend of mine, Eva Bakkeslett, has been inspired to introduce a butter-shaking dance to her bread workshops. The rhythm energises the shaking. So don't be shy! Turn on some music and shake it!

• Eventually, just as you are on the verge of giving up, the cream will separate into curds and whey, and the fats will stick together in a lump. At this point you can drain off the whey through a clean sieve. Reserve the whey for another project, and mix the fats in a bowl with a pinch of salt to taste. Pop in the fridge to stiffen. Use a couple of wooden spatulas to 'pat' the butter into shape — and feel a connection with the centuries of dairymaids and farmers' wives who've done this.

skin has not been over-stretched: loosen it with a little gentle rocking, if there is any sign of tightness or splitting.

8. Place the loaf in/on the prepared tin/tray seam side down. Spray or brush the top of the loaf with water and/or brush with beaten egg for a shiny finish. Alternatively, for rolls, place these on the prepared baking tray, about the width of three fingers apart, to allow for spreading. Leave the loaf to rise in a warm place for about 40–60 minutes. The rolls will only need about 20 minutes to rise.

9. Preheat your oven to 180°C/350°F/Gas Mark 4.

10. When the bread is ready to go into the oven, it will usually have doubled in size, completely filling the loaf tin and poking out of it by a few centimetres/an inch or so. Any sign of dimpling on the surface means it has over-risen, so rush it into the oven. It is better to put your bread in the oven when still – *just* – on the rise, so that its last burst of rising is stimulated by the heat of the oven. Bake on the middle shelf for about 45 minutes; rolls for about 20–25 minutes. Test by turning over and tapping the base, the loaf or rolls should sound hollow. Turn out and leave to cool on wire racks.

VARIATION This dough is also suitable for shaping and plaiting – see Tara's bread-knot on page 63.

INTERWEAVING & INTERCONNECTING

For meditators and bakers alike, it pays to give yourself a quiet, uninterrupted space where you can concentrate and focus consciously on what you are doing. The more practised you become, the less important that protected space is — nonetheless it is always a pleasure to give yourself the chance to dwell fully on a task.

W HEN IT COMES TO INTERWEAVING BANDS of pastry, to create a perfect latticework over a tart, or interlacing ropes of dough to create a Celtic-style bread-knot, you need to pay close attention as you perfect the technique, so allow your kitchen to become your shrine. Stick a notice on the door that says: 'Quiet, Please. Meditation in Progress!'

Such bakerly interweaving can be seen as a metaphor, or re-enactment, for the process of interconnecting that underpins our lives in so many ways. First, there is the microscopic interlacing that happens at a molecular level, when our food is cooked. Second, at the more visible level of making latticework or tying knots using dough, there is the reminder of the systemic interweaving of roles and relationships that underpins our social structure.

*For meditators and bakers alike,
it pays to give yourself a quiet,
uninterrupted space*

SPINACH & FETA LATTICE TART

In this substantial, Greek-style pie, pastry weaves itself over a cushion of dark green like a Celtic knot loosely enclosing and adorning its earthy charge. There is much more veg. – less fat, less protein, than in a quiche, making this pie a well-balanced meal in itself. You could pop it in a cake tin and take it on a picnic. But for variety at the lunch table, serve with a tomato salad, a carrot salad or a potato salad – or all three. The weaving of the pastry is easy to do – especially if you remember to start by making a cross in the middle! When preparing this meal in time for supper, I make sure that the pastry cases have been chilled in advance, and the spinach mixture given time to cool. This allows time for conscientious, enjoyable, lattice-making and baking.

Makes *1 medium tart, serving 6–8*

Preparation time 45 minutes–1 hour including cooling

Baking time 35–45 minutes

Special equipment 21-cm/8-inch loose-based cake tin with straight edges, about 5 cm/2 inches deep, greased

Ingredients

PASTRY

• 110 g/4 oz cold butter, plus extra for greasing
• 225 g/8 oz plain flour, plus extra for dusting • 2 pinches of salt • 2 tbsp sesame seeds • 2–3 tbsp cold water
• 1 tsp olive oil • Milk, beaten egg or water, for brushing

FILLING

• 750 g/1 lb 10 oz spinach or chard, trimmed weight
(900g/2 lb if frozen) • 2 medium-large onions • 1–2 tbsp olive
oil • 1 tsp Dijon mustard • 180 g/6 oz feta cheese, crumbled
• 75 g/3 oz grated mature Cheddar cheese • Salt and freshly
ground black pepper • A pinch of grated nutmeg
• 2 tbsp polenta • 1 tbsp sesame seeds

Method

1. Remove any tough-looking stems or yellow leaves from
the spinach or chard. Chop the stalks and put them in a saucepan. Add only 2–3 cm/about an inch of water to the pan to
'semi-steam' the leaves. Roughly chop the leaves and put
them on top of the stalks. Once the leaves have wilted and the
stalks are slightly softened, drain through a colander, then
place the colander in a bowl. Press gently to remove some of
the excess moisture. (If using frozen spinach, cook according
to the instructions on the packet, then leave to drain.)

2. Peel and dice the onions, then sauté in the olive oil until
soft. Add the drained and lightly pressed spinach to the onions
and leave to cool.

3. Make the pastry case. Put the flour, salt and sesame seeds
into a bowl, then grate in the butter. Mix the butter gratings
loosely into the flour then rub them between your fingertips
until the mixture resembles breadcrumbs. Add the cold water
and olive oil, blending with a wooden spoon (to prevent your

hands getting too sticky). As the liquids are absorbed, let your hands take over, pushing the dough together and kneading briefly into a smooth ball, before shaping into a fat 'frizzbee'. Pop this frizzbee on a plate that has been lightly dusted with flour, then put it in a plastic bag and chill for 15–20 minutes to rest. (If the pastry becomes too cold and stiff to handle easily, simply leave it to sit at room temperature for a few minutes before rolling out.)

4. Preheat your oven to 180°C/350°F/Gas Mark 4. On a lightly floured surface, roll the pastry out quite thinly (about 3 mm/⅛ inch thick). Now, cut a 5-cm/2-inch wide strip of pastry and place it around the inner edge of the tin, so that it bends over on to the base of the tin by about 5 mm/¼ inch. Using the base of the tin as a template cut out a round of pastry. Brush the bent-in base of the pastry wall with milk or water then fit the round piece of pastry snugly onto the base and on top of the bent-in edge of pastry, pressing it down at the edges where it overlaps. The milk or water will help 'glue' the pieces of pastry together.

5. Gather the rest of the pastry together, and roll out into a 21-cm/8-inch long rectangle (same thickness). Cut out 10 x 1-cm/½-inch wide strips of pastry. Only two of these need to be as long as the tin – the others can be a bit less.

6. Mix the cooled vegetables, mustard, crumbled feta and grated Cheddar together for the filling, then season to taste with salt, pepper and a little grated nutmeg.

7. Sprinkle the pastry case with a thin layer of polenta – this will help to absorb surplus moisture from the spinach and help prevent the pastry from becoming soggy.

8. Heap the filling into the pastry case and spread it out evenly. There should be about ½ cm/¼ inch of pastry wall still exposed. Scatter the sesame seeds over the top of the filling.

9. Now for the fun part! Place the first long strip of pastry across the middle of the tart – it should reach right up to the edge of the pastry, but must not be pressed on to it. Place the second long strip across the middle of the first so that it forms a cross (X). Next, place a strip on either side of (and parallel to) the first strip, crossing over the second strip. The fifth and sixth strips, will lie parallel to the second strip and you will have to lift up the first strip so that they can slide under it. From now on, every strip you place will require one or more previous strips to be gently lifted, so the interweaving is even, and each strip weaves alternately over and under the other strips it crosses. Keep the placing of the strips fairly loose. When the lattice is complete, trim the edges where the strips meet the pastry edge. Brush the inside of this edge with milk and turn it over the ends of the strips, so that it neatly encloses them. If you want the lattice to be shiny, brush with beaten egg, but do not let it dribble on to the spinach.

10. Bake the tart for 35–45 minutes until the pastry is golden brown and it smells cheesy and delicious. Leave to stand for 10 minutes before removing from the tin and serving.

TARA'S QUATERNARY BREAD-KNOT

My colleague, Tara Vaughan-Hughes, showed me how to make this beautiful Celtic-style knotted bread. To begin with, the ends of the dough ropes are visible, but by the time you have woven them together and tucked them underneath your knot of bread, you will no longer be able to see a beginning or an end. This seamless quality is typical of mystic knot symbols, and can remind us of the timeless nature of our spirit; the infinite cycles of birth and rebirth.

Another way to bring consciousness and love into your cooking is to chant, either aloud or to yourself. You can use a tried-and-tested mantra that you know works for you, or make up a new one. Popular phrases repeated are 'Love and light with each bite' or 'Bring health and heal with every meal'. The intention is to focus love into your food and to prevent negativity from entering your cooking. Thus, a mantra can be useful when you feel particularly vulnerable to negative emotions. Baking is your opportunity to tune into the goodness of the task at hand, and mantras can assist this tuning.

'The artist speaks to our capacity for
delight and wonder;
to our sense of fellowship with creatures;
to the invincible conviction of solidarity
that knits together all humanity.'

ADAPTED FROM JOSEPH CONRAD (1857–1924)
NOVELIST & SHORT-STORY WRITER

Makes *1 bread-knot*

Preparation time 20–30 minutes, plus 2–3 hours rising

Baking time 40–45 minutes

Special equipment 1 medium baking tray, lined with baking parchment

Ingredients

As for the light brown bread recipe on page 53.

Method

1. Make your dough according to the recipe on pages 53–57. When the dough has risen for 1 hour, you are ready to begin making the bread knot. Clean and dry a good stretch of work surface, about 1 m / 3 ft wide.

2. Divide the dough into 4 equal pieces, then roll each piece of dough into a ball, and put them on the prepared baking tray, not touching each other. As you feel each ball forming under your palms, say or think: *This sphere symbolizes eternity; no beginning, no end, each surface feeding into the next. The shape of movement and balance. (This can be simplified to: earth, moon, sun.)*

3. Next, take each ball of dough and roll it until it elongates, taking the shape of a sausage, then a cucumber, then finally a very long snake. When each piece resists (at about cucumber stage), go on to the next, then come back to the first. As you roll, you will need to slowly open your fingers to stretch the dough, at the same time moving them back and forth. Repeat this action up and down the dough as it stretches, to keep the piece even. Continue until each reaches almost 1-m/3-ft long.

4. While you are rolling the dough to elongate it, think or say: *The shape of life is changing under my fingertips; diversity is emerging. This is the transformative potential of matter that is mine too. All for the glory and resilience of our beautiful world. (This can be simplified to: change, diversify, transform.)*

5. When the four dough ropes are ready, identify them clearly as one, two, three and four by snipping both ends into 2-cm/1-inch deep 'tassles' – two tassles indicating rope two, three tassles indicating rope three, four tassles for rope four. You are now ready to begin your knot. Begin by using ropes one and two to make a simple cross – one strand of dough (rope one) placed vertically, another (rope two) crossing over its centre. *North to South; East to West. Meeting in the middle: a point of balance.*

6. Next, lay another dough rope beside the first vertical rope (rope one), on its left, crossing over the horizontal rope (rope two). *North to South; over East to West. Meeting in the middle: a point of balance.*

7. Lay your fourth dough rope below the horizontal rope (rope two), and make your first weave by lifting up your first dough rope so you can thread your fourth rope under and then, over the third rope. *East to West under (then over) North to South meeting in the middle: a point of balance. Seen and unseen surfaces of dough (as life) woven together.*

8. By now, you should have a woven double cross, with two vertical and two horizontal dough ropes. You are now going to lose sight of the compass directions, as each dough rope works its way around the central two-by-two cross, one jump at a time. Begin by moving the bottom left rope closest to you (rope three) anti-clockwise, over its neighbouring dough rope (rope one), then pick up the NEW neighbouring dough rope (rope four) and move this over its neighbour (rope two). When you've landed, again let go of the dough rope you've just moved and pick up the adjacent dough rope and cross it over its neighbour. Keep moving in one direction until you have gone full circle, then reverse your direction and go clockwise around the centre, following the same rules. Following this basic rhythm you will find that you soon use up the lengths, at which point you need only to bundle the remaining ends under the knotted cushion.

9. As you are weaving your way around, you will find that your hands learn what to do next. Thinking too hard about what you are doing can interfere with the accomplishment of the task, but to begin with, you need to observe what you are doing. On the facing page are some words to accompany the process, but don't worry if you cannot bring in a mantra.

10. To finish the loaf, spray with water and sprinkle with flour, or brush with beaten egg for a shiny finish. Leave to rise on the baking tray in a warm place for 1–2 hours, until it has almost doubled in size. Preheat your oven to 180°C/350°F/

Gas Mark 4 and bake for 40–45 minutes, or until the loaf sounds hollow when tapped on its base. Cool on a wire rack.

Crossing over we meet & greet. Say goodbye as our neighbour flies.
Crossing over we meet & greet. Say goodbye as our neighbour flies.
Crossing over we meet & greet. Say goodbye as our neighbour flies
Crossing over we meet & greet. Say goodbye as our neighbour flies.
(Reversing our journey, we step out again.)
Joy concealing sorrow.
Visible over invisible.
Matter over spirit.
Light over dark.
Ends, beginnings & boundaries merging together.

Getting Messy

Like gardeners, cooks need to be prepared to get messy, in order to get to grips with some of their ingredients. Baking gives us the opportunity to confront these undulations of orderliness without 'flipping out', and to experience them as simply a mini-cycle within a broader cycle of ongoing life.

Making this Dark Chocolate Tart with Medlars will involve getting your fingers covered in fruity mush, in order to transform a rather unusual fruit into a dessert of epicurean deliciousness. If you can't find medlars, use prunes with their stones in for a similarly rewarding culinary and mindful experience.

DARK CHOCOLATE TART
WITH MEDLARS (OR PRUNES)

After the first November frosts the olive-beige Dartington medlars are harvested and stored away, hard, astringent and inedible. A few weeks later they have 'bletted'— that is, begun to ferment, soften and turn a deep mahogany-brown. They can now be transformed into one of the most subtle desserts, for medlars combine so deliciously with chocolate that they could make an orange jealous!

The medlar is a hardy winter fruit that belongs to the rose family and is a cousin of the apple; it looks like a cross between the two — a small, dull-skinned brownish apple, shaped like a huge rosehip, with five triangular tails at the bottom descending from exposed seedboxes. It is native to Persia, but has spread throughout Europe and into Scandinavia, where it has been appreciated for its availability when most other fruits are out of season.

The unusual prune-like taste and consistency of the medlar was popular in Victorian Britain, where the fruits were brought to the table in sawdust, the brown pulp scraped out and mixed with sugar and cream. In recent years, with convenience foods holding centre-stage, the medlar has fallen from favour, but things are changing now. As we transition to a more sustainable future using the Slow Food and local food movements as our beacons, there is an open invitation to engage once again in the processing of our own seasonal winter fruit. Dealing with medlars is an earthy experience that will take you back to childhood days of mud-pie making — without the frustration of being unable to eat the end-product!

Makes *1 medium–large tart*

Preparation time 1½–2 hours, plus 20 minutes chilling

Baking time 45–55 minutes

Special equipment 28-cm/11- inch loose-based
flan tin, lightly oiled

Ingredients

FILLING

• 500 g/1 lb 2 oz whole bletted medlars, giving 350 ml/
350 g/12 fl oz medlar pulp (yielding a total mush of
600 ml/1 pint or 650 g/1 lb 7 oz when weighed) or 450 g/
1 lb whole prunes with stones • 150 ml/5 fl oz warm water,
as required • 225 g/8 oz plain chocolate, roughly chopped
• 30 g/1 oz butter • 180 ml/6 fl oz double cream or sour
cream • 110 g/4 oz golden granulated sugar • 4 beaten eggs

CHOCOLATE PASTRY

• 170 g/6 oz plain flour, plus extra for dusting • 4 tbsp cocoa
powder • 4 tbsp caster or icing sugar • 60 g/2¼ oz ground
almonds • ½ tsp ground cinnamon • A pinch of salt • 140 g/
5 oz butter • 1 egg yolk

Method

1. *Harvesting the medlar purée.* Once the medlars have 'bletted'
the flesh will be soft and you can squeeze it out of the skins
with your fingertips. If the medlars are smaller, you may need

more to achieve the desired weight. I find it easiest to squeeze the fruit from the tail end so the seed box opens up. Then pick out the seeds (which perhaps should be called 'stones' as they are quite large), counting what is normally five and collecting them in one bowl and the pulp in another. Collect the skins in a third bowl for composting. Stir the warm water in with the stones to loosen the flesh, then rub through a coarse sieve to retrieve some of the good remaining pulp. I use a clean garden, soil-sifting, sieve. Next, mix the runnier pulp with the other pulp and put this all through a slightly finer sieve to get rid of any coarse or gritty pieces from the core.

2. Alternatively, if you have lots of medlars, you can discard the seeds without rinsing off the surplus flesh from them. Just water down the pulp and rub this through a medium mesh sieve. Keep the ratio of dilution fairly constant, about 300 ml/10 fl oz water per 450–500 g/1–1 lb 2 oz of pulp – the intensity of taste and texture will be lost if the medlar pulp becomes too sloppy.

3. *If using prunes,* the harvesting process will be much simpler! Soak overnight in enough water or orange juice to just cover the fruit. The next day, cut or push out the stones. Collect the prune flesh in a bowl and purée – check you have about 600 ml/1 pint of this purée, adding a little more water or orange juice if wildly less than the required amount.

4. Now prepare the pastry case using the ingredients listed (*see page 69*) and following the instructions for the Lattice Tart pastry on pages 59–62, omitting the sesame seeds and adding the cocoa powder, sugar and ground almonds to the dry ingredients instead. Use the egg yolk and a little cold water to bind the dough together. Roll out the pastry on a lightly floured surface until it is larger than the tart tin, then roll it up around your rolling pin and carefully unroll it over the tart tin. Gently ease it into the tin, making sure the pastry goes into the corners. Trim the pastry off about 5 mm/¼ inch above the walls of the tin, then, if desired, flute around the rim by pressing the pastry between your thumb and forefinger of each hand. Put the pastry case in the fridge while you make the filling.

5. Preheat your oven to 180°C/350°F/Gas Mark 4. Melt the chocolate and butter in a heatproof bowl set over a saucepan containing approx 5 cm/2 inches of simmering water.

6. In a separate bowl, combine the fruit purée with the cream, sugar and beaten eggs, and then add the melted chocolate. Taste and adjust the sweetness if necessary. Pour the filling into the pastry case and bake for 45 minutes, or until the filling feels set when gently touched in the middle. Serve with cream or ice cream.

VARIATION Medlar purists will enjoy making this tart without the chocolate! Use a little more medlar to make up the weight and substitute the cocoa powder in the pastry with more flour, and perhaps a teaspoon or two of mixed spice or ground ginger.

RECIPES

CHAPTER THREE

BAKING FOR WELL-BEING

*The Maori concept of Hauora, or well-being,
has been compared to the four walls of a house.[1]
Each wall represents a different, interrelated
aspect that is essential to the health of the whole,
and in order to build a dwelling that has strength,
stability and symmetry, all four dimensions are needed.
These include mental and emotional well-being,
physical well-being, spiritual well-being and social
well-being. Perhaps surprisingly, the actions of growing
and baking can work to develop all four areas,
providing the roof and floor to our well-being.*

---

[1] Dr Mason Durie, Whaiora: Maori Health Development, OUP, Auckland, 1994, p.70

RISING UP

Life is not always a 'bed of roses'. In Great Britain alone there were more than 11 million people with a limiting long-term illness, impairment or disability in 2013, according to the Office for Disability. There are also people living in isolation, those who are homeless, unemployed or suffering from depression. Indeed, statistics quoted by the Mental Health Foundation suggest that every year one in four people in the UK will experience a diagnosable mental health problem.[1]

SET AGAINST THIS, THERE IS A GROWING RECOGNITION that huge therapeutic benefits can result from engaging in the basic acts of food-growing, cooking and baking. What is needed is to make these activities accessible to *everyone* – including targeted groups who will really benefit from a boost in their well-being.

In 2013 the Real Bread Campaign published a fascinating report entitled *Rising Up*. This comprehensive, well-researched document looks at who could benefit more from bread-making, who is benefiting already and how these benefits come about. Included is a list of many inspirational organizations that use bread-baking to benefit groups as diverse as those suffering from Alzheimer's, victims of torture, ex-offenders, people with learning disabilities and those with mental-health issues. The report also touches on how the

[1] As quoted in *Rising Up*, Chris Young, Real Bread Campaign/Sustain, 2013

benefits of bread-baking can be extended to involve more people, both as trainers and as practitioners, so it is worth looking up the Real Bread Campaign and getting involved!

One of the great things about baking bread is that it is highly accessible. Very little is needed, in terms of ingredients, space and equipment. You can even do away with a bowl and an oven, by mixing together flour on a table and making flatbreads in a pan on a hob, or even over a small outdoor fire.

Mental, Physical & Social Benefits

The therapeutic benefits of bread-baking work on many levels. To knead dough we must use a wide range of movements, possess good muscle strength and have sound balance. We need to be able to judge proportions, as we divide and measure the dough, and focus on getting the timing right, which helps us concentrate. There's also a sense of accomplishment when a successful bake emerges from the oven that

---

'Doing things for others isn't only good for
them and a good thing to do, it also makes us happier
and healthier too. Giving also connects us to others,
creating stronger communities and helping
build a happier society for everyone.'

'10 KEYS TO HAPPIER LIVING, ACTION 1'
ACTION FOR HAPPINESS, REGISTERED CHARITY, UK

◆

'Slow-releasing – or complex – carbohydrates,
in foods like wholegrains, vegetables and beans, take
longer to digest than refined equivalents such as white
bread, processed cereals and sugar that have, in a sense,
been 'pre-digested' by the processing techniques.
Choosing foods that take longer to be converted
from their raw state to glucose means that your
brain receives a more stable and consistent flow
of fuel with which to function.'

FROM 'FEEDING MINDS' BY D. CORNAH
MENTAL HEALTH FOUNDATION, UK, 2006

◆

---

cannot be underestimated. Furthermore, in these days of pot-luck dinners and bake-sales, the opportunity to give and share bread may open the doors to an expanded social network.

When it comes to nutrition, engaging in bread-baking offers us a useful opportunity to explore wholegrain food. Hopefully this will lead to a lifelong appreciation of the virtues of wholefood, which will bring rewards in terms of enhanced physical well-being. Wholemeal bread contains a range of micronutrients (zinc, magnesium, B vitamins, folate, vitamin E and iron) that form part of the 'combination of nutrients that is most commonly associated with good mental health and well-being', according to Courtney Van de Weyer in his 2005 report *Changing Diets, Changing Minds*.

Of course it's easy to say that everyone should convert to a wholefood diet, but the reality is not so straightforward. Many people are very attached to their white-bread diet, and a negative experience of wholefood has put some people off. Over the years I have noted the different responses to a sudden exposure to 100 per cent wholewheat bread; as a result I have made the College's staple bread 60 per cent wholewheat and 40 per cent white unbleached flour. Nowadays we make all our own bread on the premises, but some years ago we used to buy in 100 per cent wholewheat bread from a local organic baker. When I mentioned the problem that some visitors were complaining they were getting tummy upsets from the high-fibre bread, the baker advised me that this would calm down after a few weeks and that a period of adaptation was needed. But time is not readily available when people come to the College on short courses, although I have always remembered the baker's advice. It has been a great help when it comes to understanding the ups and downs that may occur as people journey towards a healthier wholefood, high-fibre, diet.

Many people are very attached to their white-bread diet, and a negative experience of wholefood has put some people off

LIGHTENING UP

◆

There are times when a real heaviness can set in: one thing after another goes wrong and we feel as if we are living under a black cloud. Sometimes the problems that weigh us down and threaten to make life unendurable are external and physical: flooding, famine, death, tsunami, an oppressive regime.

A T OTHER TIMES WE MAY APPEAR to have a favourable environment in which to live – a nice home, plenty of food, a good job, and so on – but we become entrenched in a cycle of dissatisfaction and self-depreciation, which creates a feedback loop that makes us more and more unhappy. Relationship problems, instead of getting better, may become (or simply seem) worse.

As I have already mentioned, baking has been used to treat depression by encouraging relaxation, creating a diversion and giving an opportunity to share the results (thus encouraging social interaction). However, this isn't the whole story: baking also allows you to be creative and to identify yourself with an alternative reality – you put a bit of yourself into your baking and, on one level, you *become* your easy-rising bread, cake or scone. The following two recipes, which use a quick-acting raising agent, hold up a mirror of lightness to us, as the mixtures bubble up and set in the oven. However fleeting, this invites a form of transference.

CHEESE & CHIVE SCONES

*Warm cheese scones, torn apart in the hand and spread with butter,
or heaped with hummus, make a perfect alternative to bread at
lunchtime. They are quick to make, and because the leavening agent
is baking powder, not yeast, they don't need any proving time, so
they can be thrown together in half an hour just before you eat.*

Makes *12–15 scones*

Preparation time 10 minutes

Baking time 15–20 minutes

Special equipment 6-cm/2½-inch round pastry cutter (or
use a tumbler dipped in plain flour); 1 baking tray, dusted
lightly with flour

Ingredients

• 350 g/12 oz plain flour, plus extra for dusting • 1 tbsp
baking powder • ¼ tsp bicarbonate of soda • ½ tsp salt
• 85 g/3 oz cold butter, plus extra to serve • 10–20 fresh
chives, snipped • 175 g/6 oz grated Cheddar cheese • 1 egg
• 1 tbsp natural yogurt or use more milk • ½ tsp English
mustard • 300 ml/10 fl oz whole milk, plus extra for brushing

Method

1. Preheat your oven to 200°C/400°F/Gas Mark 6.

2. Mix the flour, baking powder, bicarbonate of soda and salt
together in a bowl. Grate or cut the butter into the flour and

rub it in with your fingertips until a breadcrumb-like consistency is obtained. Keep lifting your fingers several inches above the mixture as you rub the butter in and enjoy the snow-like falling of crumbs back into the bowl.

3. Use a pair of scissors to snip the chives into small pieces each only a few millimetres long – this can be done directly over the flour bowl, letting the chive pieces flutter down like leaves falling on a windy day. Next, mix in two-thirds of the grated cheese. Make a well in the middle of the mixture.

4. Beat the egg, yogurt and mustard into the milk then pour the mixture into the well. You may not need it all, so go cautiously, stirring with a wooden spoon, until all the crumbs are combined to form a sticky, but not sloppy dough. Press into a ball, but avoid the kind of vigorous kneading you would give bread dough, because your warm hands will melt the butter.

5. Place the dough on a floured surface. Lightly flour the top of the dough and roll out to approx. 2 cm/1 inch thick. Cut into rounds with the pastry cutter or use the tumbler, if you don't have a cutter, or cut into squares. Squash together the remaining dough and repeat until it's all used up. Place the scones on the prepared baking tray about 2 cm/1 inch apart. Brush with milk or any remaining milk/egg mix and sprinkle each one with the remaining one third of grated cheese.

6. Bake for 15–20 minutes until well risen, beginning to turn golden brown on top (and bottom) and the irresistible smell of cheese wafts around your kitchen. Serve warm with butter.

SPONGY BUFFINS

And now for something sweeter . . . These spongy banana muffins are light and airy, and have been designed to rise voluminously in the oven!

Makes *12 buffins*

Preparation time 15–20 minutes

Baking time 20–25 minutes

Special equipment 12-hole muffin tin; 12 deep paper muffin cases; 4 medium-large mixing bowls; egg whisk

Ingredients

• 3 eggs • 50 g / 2 oz golden caster sugar • 50 g / 2 oz light muscovado sugar • 150 g / 5 ½ oz plain flour • 2 tsp baking powder • ½ tsp bicarbonate of soda • 2 bananas • 3 tbsp orange juice (about ½ orange) or use water or milk
• 25 g / 1 oz butter or margarine, melted • Pinch of salt

Method

1. Preheat your oven to 190°C / 375°F / Gas Mark 5 and put the paper muffin cases into the muffin tray.

2. Separate the eggs. Put the whites in a large bowl and set aside for later. Put the egg yolks in another large bowl and add the sugar, then set aside.

3. Mix the flour, baking powder and bicarbonate of soda together in another large bowl and set aside.

4. In a separate bowl, mash the bananas and set aside.

5. Beat the yolks and sugar together with a whisk until pale and creamy. The mixture will thicken and gain volume. Add the orange juice and continue whisking for a few more minutes. Scrape the surplus off the whisk into the bowl. Wash and dry your whisk and shake it to remove any surplus water.

6. Melt the butter gently in your smallest saucepan, taking it off the heat when almost melted.

7. Whisk the egg whites with the cleaned whisk. As the bubbles begin to form add the salt and continue to whisk until the whites are fluffed up forming snowy peaks like meringue or shaving foam.

8. Now the time has come to act briskly. Mix the melted butter and mashed bananas into the beaten egg yolk and sugar using a wooden spoon. Next, fold in the flour mixture.

9. Finally, fold in the whisked egg white, adding only about half to begin with, giving it a few encorporating folds and then adding the rest. The resulting batter should have a light marshmallowy consistency. Don't beat – you want to preserve as many bubbles as possible as these will contribute to the rising of the buffins.

10. Spoon the mixture into the muffin cases, filling each just over halfway, then whizz the tray into the middle of the oven and bake for about 20–25 minutes until the buffins are well risen and golden.

11. When ready, take the buffins out of the muffin trays and leave to cool on a wire rack.

Overcoming Attachment

Do not mind too much when things go wrong and your food gets burnt, doesn't rise, or you accidentally add too much salt. In Buddhist teachings, attachment to anything represents one of the greatest obstacles to the development of your spiritual path. It is something I see in myself time and time again, manifesting as a reluctance to let go, accept my mistakes and move on. These characteristics are a vice that can hold you in a trap – but the pitfalls of baking help you to practise the art of severing these attachments. Return to this thought whenever a recipe turns out a little less successfully than you had hoped.

Metamorphosis: the Dance of Planetary Recycling

Some of the most delicious food is made from leftovers. The key thing is to recognize when the time has come to reincarnate food, before anything goes mouldy. By reusing old or abandoned ingredients, not only are we being ecological, in the sense that we are recycling rather than using anew, we are experiencing the age-old power of metamorphosis. Using lovely leftovers – as in this next recipe, a classic bread-and-butter pudding – reminds us that there is no end to metamorphosis: everything moves into a new shape, punctuated only momentarily by golden moments of stillness.

BREAD-&-BUTTER PUDDING

The Schumacher College bread bin in the snack area often needs sorting out. What with people who abandon crusts, and those who like them so much that they cut both loaf-ends off at once, making the last few pieces difficult to slice, we often have quite a lot of stale bread to use up. It is collected in a bag in the freezer until there is enough to make another type of food for 50 people. Bread-and-butter pudding is a delicious and traditional way of turning such scraps into a wholesome and economical dessert. It can be served on its own, or taken to more fanciful extremes by accompanying it with single cream, ice cream or stewed fruit.

Serves *6–8*

Preparation time 15–20 minutes

Baking time 30–40 minutes

Special equipment 1.2-litre/2-pint deep baking dish, generously greased with butter

Ingredients

• Not more than 50 g/2 oz butter, for spreading on the bread, plus extra for greasing • 8 slices white and/or brown bread • 50 g/2 oz raisins or sultanas • 25 g/1 oz unsulphured apricots, chopped • 300 ml/10 fl oz milk
• 4 tbsp cream • 50 g/1½ oz light muscovado sugar • 3 eggs
• ½ tsp finely grated lemon rind • Nutmeg, for sprinkling
• 4 tbsp apricot jam

Method

1. Preheat your oven to 180°C / 350°F / Gas Mark 4.

2. Cut the bread into medium-thick slices. Butter these and then cut in half. No need to remove the crusts. *As you are preparing the bread, think back through its journey to becoming bread, its infancy in the golden wheat fields, its processing and its sojurn in the bread bin. And remember how it almost became toast!*

3. Line the base of the prepared baking dish with a layer of buttered bread – buttered side uppermost. Sprinkle with half of the raisins or sultanas and chopped apricots and cover with another layer of bread. Toss the remaining dried fruit over this and cover with a final layer of bread.

4. Mix the milk and cream together in a large bowl. Add the sugar and the eggs and whisk until smooth. *Then* stir in the finely grated lemon rind – which can stick to the whisk if it is added earlier than this stage.

5. Pour the eggy mixture over the bread, covering it completely and allowing it to dribble through the layers. Grate some fresh nutmeg over the top and bake on the middle shelf of the oven for 30–40 minutes until golden brown colours the top and it is no longer wet.

6. Remove the pudding from the oven and spoon on the apricot jam. Spread it out to cover the whole of the top and then return to the oven for 5 minutes, so that the jam sets, covering the bread-and-butter pudding with a delicious fruity glaze. Serve warm.

Problem-Solving

Sometimes the problems we encounter in our baking can be easily resolved if we 'think outside the box' – it just takes a bit of ingenuity, adjustment and openness to change track. The solution may be as simple as changing your baking dish or altering the temperature of your oven. At other times you may need to make an unlikely substitution, bulk up your quantities as five unexpected guests arrive for lunch, or even scrape away a burnt layer and completely reinvent what you are doing. It is frequently at such moments that brilliant new recipes are born!

Seen from this perspective, the problems we encounter when we cook can have hidden benefits: they challenge our intellect, like a good crossword puzzle, as well as challenge our emotions. For if we remain stubbornly intent on starting again and following our original dream we may be left with a lot of waste – and a great deal of extra work. Better to set aside the dream for the next time, focus on plan B and move on.

Patience

Our Western consumer lifestyle encourages the 'want it all now' approach. It's as if the media culture in which we find ourselves ever more deeply entrenched is feeding us mind-food that keeps us perpetually aged 15, perpetually impatient

to get what we want straight away. On the one hand, technology has opened doors for greater freedom of movement, the quicker processing of manufactured goods and ever-faster communication. On the other hand, we have lost quality time as we rush between A and B and expect instant fixes. The art of nurturing our hopes has been usurped by the psychology of wanting – the desperate inner yearning that preys upon our insecurity and is the other face of absence.

Looking back on the recent history of bread-making, the Chorleywood 'revolution' epitomizes the drive towards quick-fixes. Not only did the Chorleywood Baking Process reduce bread-making time to a few hours, it turned it into something that had to be done in a factory, taking the personal engagement with Slow Food out of our ordinary lives.

In stark contrast to the CBP (or indeed to using a soda-based raising agent or traditional yeast), creating your own leaven or rye starter can take several days, and preparing sourdough bread several hours. Yet when we consider the health benefits of this slow bread and learn to accommodate its pattern into our daily routine, our patience will be rewarded.

The Tradition of Leaven Bread

As I mentioned in the introduction, artisan bread-making is spreading across the UK, North America and Australia, reaffirming the age-old tradition of leaven breads, which quite literally continued to bubble and ferment in Europe while a

Dark Age for bread was occurring elsewhere. Now people all over the world are taking up the Real Bread baton. More and more people are able to enjoy the health benefits of sourdough, in which the presence of lactic acid (indicative of its 'pre-digested' state) makes it easier for some people to digest. Small-scale sourdough bakeries have been opened by artisan bakers, some of whom also teach. In the us, such bakeries have been developing over the last 20 years – Dan Leader's Bread Alone Bakery in New York produces thousands of loaves a day, while its owner also teaches. Increasingly bread is being made at home – often with bread-making machines providing a transition between buying bread in shops and getting really hands-on by baking from scratch.

A few years ago Andrew Whitley, the hugely effective baker-turned-Real-Bread-campaigner, came to teach at Schumacher College. We were immediately inspired as Andrew got us 'air-kneading' (pulling dough back and forth between our raised hands) and mixing a Russian rye sourdough to the perfect 'mud-pie' consistency. At the close of his baking lesson, rye starter that had been acquired some 30 years ago in Russia was distributed to anyone who asked for some (leaven can last for decades, and while the percentage of the original leaven is diluted, its potency remains). We have nurtured our own little pot of grey goo by frequent use and have given tiny jars of it away on many occasions. As a result, what began as Andrew's Russian leaven is now spreading all round

Totnes. However, we also discovered that the Whitley recipe for making leaven from scratch works well, and so, provided you have the time, it isn't always necessary to get your baker friends to send plastic bags of leaven through the post! I recently emailed a recipe to a former student who was missing the College's Borodinsky rye bread while studying overseas. A couple of weeks later he sent me photos of himself proudly holding loaves that he'd made using the recipe for leaven given below. The bread had turned out beautifully.

Making your own leaven from scratch – at least once – will give you a deeper insight into the sourdough process, which has fermentation at its heart. As a lesson in patience, making your own leaven is exemplary, because it will take you *even* longer to get to the point where you can bake your first loaf of bread. You will need more patience – so there is even less attachment to instant results.

What is Fermentation?

Fermentation is the chemical change of a substance brought about by bacteria, yeasts, moulds or other microorganisms. It is normally accompanied by effervescence and the giving-off of heat. Examples are found in the souring of milk, the conversion of sugar to alcohol, the pickling of cabbage in sauerkraut and the rising of dough.

MINDFULNESS IN BAKING

CREATING YOUR OWN
SOURDOUGH STARTER (LEAVEN)

(based on Andrew Whitley's recipe in Bread Matters *(2009))*
If you don't have a leaven, or access to one, you'll need to make your own, beginning a week before. That's just on the first occasion – from then on you'll be able to keep the leaven in your fridge, replenishing it every time you bake, or every week (whichever is the more frequent). All you'll need is flour, water, warmth, air and time.

Makes *approx 300 g / 10 oz sourdough starter for leavening bread*
Preparation time 4–6 days, depending on ambient temperature
Special equipment 1 container (e.g. 500 ml / 18 fl oz lidded kilner jar or plastic pot or bowl with plate on top); thermometer (optional)

Method

Find a warm spot, such as a shelf near a radiator, or cooker, or on top of your fridge to ferment your starter – 28–30°C / 82—86°F is ideal and will encourage natural yeasts to operate at their maximum level of reproductivity.

DAY ONE Combine • 25 g / 1 oz organic rye flour • 4 tbsp warm water at 40°C / 104°F
Mix the rye flour and warm water to a sloppy paste. A bowl with a plate on top, or kilner-style jar (not clipped down) can

be used for this. Using organic rye flour is ideal for creating a starter because it contains more wild yeast and bacteria than other types of flour.

DAY TWO Add • 25 g / 1 oz wholemeal (dark) rye flour
4 tbsp warm water at 40°C / 104°F • Starter from Day 1
Stir the fresh flour and water into the mixture, cover and return to a warm place.

DAY THREE Add • 25 g / 1 oz organic rye flour • 4 tbsp warm water at 40°C / 104°F • Starter from Days 1 and 2
Stir the fresh flour and warm water into the starter, which may now show signs of frothing.

DAY FOUR Add • 25 g / 1 oz wholemeal (dark) rye flour
4 tbsp warm water at 40°C / 104°F • Starter from Days 1, 2 and 3 (300 g / 10½ oz total weight)
Mix the fresh flour and warm water into the starter. By the following day, Andrew says 'you should have a sourdough that has bubbled up and subsided and smells fruity. If you dip a finger in and lick it, the sour [mixture] should taste mildly acidic.' If your starter shows no signs of life after Day 5, repeat the additions of Day 4 – it probably needs a little longer to get going. Store your starter in a container with the lid loosely fitted, as leavens can get very lively and swell up. Never fill your container more than two thirds of the way to the top!

RYE-WHEAT SOURDOUGH BREAD

Once you have cultivated your leaven, you'll be ready to take on any sourdough challenge. The basic rye starter or leaven can be adapted for use in other breads by adding white or brown wheat flour. I keep a starter in our fridge, which I refresh with water, white flour and rye flour every time I bake our favourite home loaf, a light rye sourdough. Because I use the leaven a couple of times a week I never have to worry about feeding it. If you're leaving it for more than a couple of weeks, either freeze or feed your starter to keep it lively and prevent it becoming sour to the point of acidity. To feed it, follow the same technique as for refreshing your starter, but use just half the ingredients. Compost the surplus starter or use it in regular yeasted bread-making to add a little sourdough flavour. If you want to make two or three loaves, the same amount of starter can be used to refresh up to three times the amount of flour and water given for one loaf.

Special equipment 1-litre/approx 2-pint ceramic bowl for day one; 1.1 kg/2½ lb loaf tin, lightly oiled with sunflower oil for day two.

DAY ONE Refreshing your starter (allow 12–18 hours)

Ingredients
- 70 g/2½ oz plain unbleached organic white flour
- 50 g/2 oz rye flour • 250 ml/9 fl oz warm water
- About 200 g/7 oz leaven

Mix the flour, warm water and leaven together in the bowl until smooth. There should be a good 6–8-cm/2½–3-inch gap between the leaven and the top of the bowl. Clean the sides with a spatula. Cover with a saucer. Leave this at room temperature for at least 12 hours) during which time the starter will rise and fall, doubling its volume in between.

DAY TWO Making your sourdough (allow 5–8 hours)

Ingredients
• 100 g/3½ oz rye flour • 300 g/10½ oz white, organic unbleached flour, plus extra for dusting • 200 g/7 oz refreshed starter (*see pages 90–92*) • 200 ml/7 fl oz warm water • 1 rounded tsp salt • 1 tbsp honey • A little olive oil

1. Mix all the ingredients, except the olive oil, together into a fairly stiff, porridgey dough. It will be wet to touch, but not runny. Put the surplus starter back in the fridge for next time.
2. Leave the dough to rise for 1 hour, then turn out and knead using a little olive oil or flour to stop it sticking. (I turn my dough onto a wooden tray so I can move it out of the way if I need to). Leave to rise for a further 1–2 hours. Knead again for only 15 seconds. Repeat this process once more if time.
3. Knead and shape into a cocoon, with the joints pressed under, the top smooth. Leave in the loaf tin. Spray or splash with water, then brush oil over the top and leave to rise at

room temperature for several hours until doubled in size. (Alternatively, for a more rustic look, leave to rise in a floured tea towel in a bowl, then upturn onto a baking tray to bake. This simulates a 'bannaton' which is the term used for the baskets artisan bakers use to prove round and oval loaves. These are now readily available in cookshops and online).

4. Preheat your oven to 180°C/350°F/Gas Mark 4 and bake the loaf for about 45–50 minutes. When ready, the bread will sound hollow when knocked on the base. Turn out and cool on a wire rack.

I am always so delighted when my sourdough has risen well and the first slice reveals the bouncy air holes laced together by a well-developed network of glutenous threads; everything stopped in its tracks by heat at just the right moment. Had the proving gone on any longer, they might have subsided; any shorter and the air holes would have been smaller, and less welcoming as pockets for butter, olive oil and jam.

Although I bake sourdough a couple of times a week, the magic of baking without yeast always gives me a great thrill, and the deeper taste it offers is always worth waiting for. Knowing that you have created the potent raising agent is awe-inspiring. If your bread is not perfect, but tastes good, this is your invitation to make it again and again.

Hidden Treasures

Life is full of surprises, and sometimes it pays to wait and see if things really are what you think they are, before you panic or make a hasty judgement. Bite carefully and chew well, savouring the experience and using all your senses to give you a deeper taste of what is being revealed. In this next recipe you are concealing 'treasure', in the form of a layer of marzipan buried in an enriched dough. Those you share this with will be pleasantly surprised, and reminded that the unexpected can often be welcome.

TREASURE STOLLEN

This very special, and occasional, loaf is a rich, fruity, marzipan-filled bread that originated in Dresden, Germany. Its sugar-dusted, elongated shape is thought to have a particular relevance to its traditional role as a Christmas delicacy — its appearance represents the baby Jesus wrapped in swaddling bands. In this recipe, I have added some plain chocolate chunks to the fruit mix, bringing extra jewels to the treasure trove.

Makes *1 large, cocoon-shaped loaf*

Preparation time 1 hour, plus 8 hours soaking and 1½–2 hours rising

Baking time 35–45 minutes

Special equipment 1 baking tray, lined with baking parchment

Ingredients

FRUIT MIX FOR SOAKING

• 25 g / 1 oz currants • 25 g / 1 oz sultanas • 25 g / 1 oz raisins
• 25 g / 1 oz mixed peel, chopped • 50 g / 2 oz natural glacé
cherries, halved • Zest and 3 tbsp juice of 1 organic orange
• 65 ml / 2½ fl oz / 5 tbsp dark rum or brandy • 100 g / 3½ oz
plain chocolate, at least 70% cocoa solids, roughly chopped

ENRICHED DOUGH

• 400 g / 14 oz strong white flour • ¼ tsp salt • ½ tsp grated
nutmeg • 1 tsp mixed spice • 2 tsp dried yeast or 15 g / ½ oz
fresh yeast, crumbled • 125 g / 4½ oz butter • 150 ml / 5 fl oz
warm milk • 50 g / 2 oz golden caster sugar • 2 eggs • 2–3 tbsp
rum or brandy

MARZIPAN

• 125 g / 4½ oz ground almonds • 85 g / 3 oz icing sugar,
sifted, plus extra for dusting • ¼ tsp pure natural almond
extract (optional) • A little egg white to bind (2–3 tbsp)

DECORATION

• 2–3 tbsp flaked almonds • 1–2 tbsp icing sugar, sifted
• 1–2 tsp cocoa powder, sifted

Method

1. Combine the dried fruit with the orange zest, juice and rum or brandy in a jar with a lid. Leave to steep overnight. The next day, add the chopped chocolate to the brew.

2. To make the dough, combine the flour, salt and spices (if using fast-acting dried yeast, add at this stage too).

3. Next, melt two-thirds of the butter (75 g / 3 oz) with the milk in a saucepan. Stir in the sugar until dissolved. Cool.

4. When the liquid is just warm, stir in the fresh yeast or traditional dried yeast and mix until dissolved.

5. Separate 1 egg, putting the white carefully aside to make the marzipan later. Whisk the remaining whole egg and the egg yolk into the yeasty milk mixture.

6. Make a well in the middle of the flour and pour in the wet ingredients. Mix with a wooden spoon, then let your floured hands take over at a point where they will not get too sticky. Knead gently until fairly smooth in the bowl or on a floured surface. Spray the surface of the dough and leave to rise in the bowl in a warm (not draughty) place for 1½–2 hours.

7. Meanwhile, prepare the marzipan by mixing together the ground almonds, icing sugar, almond extract and as much of the reserved egg white as required to give a soft kneadable consistency (2–3 tbsp). Dust your work surface with icing sugar and roll the marzipan into a fat sausage about the length of your baking tray (about 30 cm / 12 inches long), then flatten into a rectangle, about 1½ cm / ¾ inch thick and set aside.

8. In a small pan, melt together the remaining one third of butter with the rum or brandy.

9. Returning to the dough (which can be left for up to 3 hours, if convenient, as enriched doughs are slower to rise), place it on to a lightly floured work surface and 'knock back' with a little kneading. Begin to roll out into a rectangle about 1 cm / ½ inch thick. If the dough resists rolling, let it rest for a few moments and then go back to it. As the gluten relaxes, the elasticity will reduce making it easier to roll out further.

10. Brush your rectangle of dough all over with the melted butter-rum mixture, then spread half of the fruit and chocolate mix on to the bottom two thirds of the dough, leaving a margin round the edge. Next, fold the 'naked' top third down over the fruity middle third, covering it. Continue by folding the whole middle section over onto the bottom third. Press the surface lightly with your hand to ease out any air, and pinch the ends together to seal. Turn the dough so that the short ends now face vertically up and down, then roll out into a rectangle, brush, cover two thirds with fruity mix and fold.

11. Roll out the dough again, brush and place the marzipan rectangle down the centre of the dough. *You are hiding our treasure for the delight of all seekers...* Fold the two long sides over it so they meet at the centre, either slightly overlapping or pinched together. The ends can also be pinched together or left to merge together in the oven. Put the Stollen carefully, joint-side down, onto the baking tray and brush with more

melted butter and rum. Scatter with the flaked almonds and leave to rise in a warm place for 30 minutes.

12. Preheat your oven to 180°C/350°F/Gas Mark 4. Bake the Stollen for 35–45 minutes until lightly brown. The underside will sound hollowish when tapped.

13. Remove the Stollen from the oven and brush with the remaining reheated rum and butter mixture, then dust with icing sugar rubbed through a sieve. (A good snowy dredging is traditional, but it is not always well received by health conscious Schumacher College people, so I usually sprinkle the Stollen minimally at this point). Leave to cool before serving, with a final sifting of icing sugar followed by cocoa.

By popular request, I bake Stollen for tea almost every Christmas. My husband – who is convinced that hiding coins in Christmas puddings is a dangerous, completely barmy English habit that is liable to cause choking and teeth-breakages – prefers the soft treasures of Stollen. Because I always make two, there is usually a Stollen left to be shared in January when the students arrive back at the College. I always love it when someone who has never eaten Stollen before cuts a slice and is surprised: 'What is that?' (pointing to the marzipan). 'And that?' (tasting it). 'Mmm, chocolate!' (as they come across the treasure). 'Do you mind if I have another slice?'

RECIPES

CHAPTER FOUR

BAKING FOR ENLIGHTENMENT

*Baking can become an entirely absorbing,
wave-riding pastime. Indeed, it is an activity
that can let us experience that fully immersive
and energized engagement with a task that has been
described by the Hungarian psychology professor
Mihaly Csikszentmihalyi as 'flow'. In addition, we can
use baking as a springboard for scientific exploration,
and as a means of exercising our own ability to reason
and find explanations. As the German philosopher
Immanuel Kant said, in answer to the question
'What is enlightenment?': 'Have courage to use
your own reason! That is the motto
of enlightenment'.*

TRANSFORMATION

◆

All kinds of cooking are transformative. Often the transformation happens within the depths of the oven, hidden from view, but at other times it happens before our very eyes, amazing and enthralling us in equal measure.

V ERY OFTEN IN BAKING, AS IN LIFE, we become the transformers of something in nature that was intended for another purpose entirely. We carve spoons from branches ripped from trees, use their leaves as plates, and take our sustenance from the nutrition-rich early food or life-forms of other animals and plants. We are part of a food chain that links together plants, animals and sunlight in an inter-dependent web of being, so it is not surprising that our way of survival reflects this capacity to take from elsewhere in nature and to be immensely creative with our scavengings.

Culinary Shape-Shifting

The radical change in structure that occurs when egg whites are whisked must surely be one of the most remarkable shape-shifting events to confront any culinary dabbler or professional. Egg whites become a practical metaphor for metamorphosis.

At a chemical level, what happens when we whisk egg whites is that the physical stress of dragging the gooey liquid

through itself with the beater forces the protein molecules to unfold. At the same time, by mixing air into the whites, the proteins are forced out of their natural state. These denatured proteins gather together and create multiple bonds with the other unravelled proteins, thus forming a foam that holds the incorporated air in place. This process of coagulation occurs because the proteins consist of amino acids, some of which are attracted to water (hydrophilic) and others repelled by water (hydrophobic). On a visible level, what we notice is that the foam becomes gradually stiffer, which is why cooks identify three stages: soft, firm peaks, followed by stiff peaks and then overbeaten whites, which take on a dry, almost grainy appearance and eventually collapse. But watch out that you don't allow any form of fat or oil into the bowl. Even the fats contained in the egg yolk will be enough to prevent the egg whites from whisking up nicely.

Set alongside this rationalized description of what happens when egg whites are whipped is the sheer amazement of transformation, which makes working with egg whites a time of fun (and elbow grease!). I often wonder who first discovered a culinary advantage in a particular ingredient, or fusion of ingredients, and by what accident this happened. Perhaps the trick – like the whipping of egg whites – popped up in different places all over the world and then, by some 'hundredth-monkey principle', spread like wildfire, aerating meringues, cakes and soufflés across a continent …

CHEESE & PUMPKIN SOUFFLÉ

Concocting a soufflé is fun! The sight of the whipped egg whites is quite spectacular — especially when cooking for 50 (as I frequently do). Just like the clouds in the sky, a bowl of breathy egg-white fluff is (both literally and artistically) an in-spire-ation to behold! You'll need your eaters to be punctual, and then, like cloud, your soufflé will sit proudly holding its shape just long enough to be appreciated — until north winds, or knives and forks, whisk it away.

Serves 6

Preparation time about 45 minutes

Baking time 35–40 minutes

Special equipment 25-cm/10-inch round baking dish, 10 cm/4 inches deep, generously greased with butter

Ingredients

• 25 g/1 oz butter, plus extra for greasing • 300 g/10 oz good orange-fleshed winter squash • A little olive oil • 2–3 pinches of salt • 150 g/5 oz Cheddar cheese • 250 ml/9 fl oz milk • 5 eggs • 30 g/1 oz plain flour • Pinch of freshly ground black pepper • Pinch of nutmeg • 1 tsp mustard • 1 tbsp chopped fresh parsley • 1 tbsp pumpkin seeds

Method

1. Preheat your oven to 190°C/375°F/Gas Mark 5. Cut the squash into wedges, peel and deseed. Next, cut the flesh into

small chunks, about 1–1½ cm / ½–¾-inch square. Set 60 g / 2¼ oz aside for steaming. Toss the rest in olive oil and spread out on a baking tray. Sprinkle with a pinch of salt and cook in the oven for about 20–25 minutes until just soft. Steam the reserved squash until soft (about 15–20 minutes).

2. Grate the cheese and scatter about 3 tablespoons on the base of your prepared dish. Make sure that you can still see the base of the dish peeping through. Scatter the roasted squash chunks over the top.

3. Pour the milk into a blender, add the steamed squash and blitz until you have a sort of squash 'smoothie'. Alternatively, mash the squash with a fork, then press the squash through a sieve and mix with the milk.

4. Separate the eggs, putting the whites in a large glass bowl.

5. Gently melt the butter in a large pan, then stir in the flour to form a roux. Add a little of the pumpkin milk, and stir until smooth, then add a little more. Add the rest stirring regularly, then remove from the heat and stir in the remaining grated cheese. Season with the salt, pepper, nutmeg and mustard and leave the mixture to cool for 10 minutes.

6. Just 5–10 minutes before you need to put your soufflé in the oven, whisk the reserved egg whites until they form frothy white peaks that stack up and hold their shape well – like cumulous clouds. It is very important to get your timing just right here – so start whisking the egg whites 50 minutes before you need to serve the soufflé.

7. Now act quickly. Stir the egg yolks and parsley into the cheese sauce, then gently fold in the whisked egg white, half or a third at a time with a wide spatula.

8. When the egg white has been evenly folded in and is well distributed, (but not beaten at all – because you want to preserve as many bubbles as possible), pour the marshmallowy mixture into the baking dish. There should be at least 6 cm/2½ inches of side still exposed to support it as it rises, and at least a third of this should be the wall of the dish – rather than an extension you can make with baking parchment (which isn't as strong). Typically the soufflé will double in size, so the mixture should be about 6 cm/2½ inches deep before it goes in the oven.

9. Toss the pumpkin seeds over the top and place the soufflé on the middle shelf of the oven, making sure there are no overhanging racks that will obstruct it during rising. Put your timer on for 40 minutes. Cook for the first 30 minutes without peeping, then very gently open the oven door and check all is going well. Slide gently around if one side is browning more quickly than another, but avoid actually removing from oven. Close the door *gently* to finish cooking. The soufflé is ready to be rushed to the table when well risen, golden brown on top and set evenly in its own uniquely spongy way. A depression in the middle may indicate that this area is still under cooked – if unsure, test with a skewer. If it comes out very gooey, allow 5–10 minutes longer in the oven.

FOREST-FRUITS PAVLOVA

Before we finish dancing with egg whites, let's explore what happens when stiffly whipped egg white is combined with fine sugar. When baked at a low temperature, the sugar stiffens the white in the oven, helping to maintain its whipped shape and foamy appearance. As it dries out, the brittle confection that we know as meringue emerges. The original Pavlova dessert was created in honour of the Russian ballerina Anna Pavlova, when she visited New Zealand in 1926. Crisp on the outside and light and soft on the inside, it was the answer to her dessert dreams – and Pavlova has remained the national dish of Australia and New Zealand ever since.

Serves *8 (1 big dinner plate-sized Pavlova)*

Preparation time 30 minutes before baking

Baking time 3 hours, plus 20–30 minutes cooling

Special equipment 1 medium baking tray lined with baking parchment, very lightly oiled and then lightly dusted with cornflour, with the excess cornflour tipped out; 1 large piping bag with a 2-cm/¾-inch wide nozzle or a large metal spoon

Ingredients

MERINGUE

• ½ tsp sunflower oil for the tray • 2–3 tsp cornflour for the tray • 225 g/8 oz caster sugar • 4 eggs • Pinch of salt • ¼ tsp ground cinnamon

FILLING

• 300 g / 10½ oz fresh raspberries, redcurrants, blueberries
and strawberries OR the same amount of frozen forest
berries with 100 ml / 3½ fl oz apple juice, 2 tsp arrowroot
and 1 tbsp sugar or agave syrup • 500–600 ml / 18 fl oz–1
pint whipping cream • 1 tsp caster sugar (optional) • A fresh
mint sprig or a few plain chocolate shavings, 2–3 tbsp lightly
toasted flaked almonds or edible flowers, such as violas,
primroses or rose petals, to decorate (optional)

Method

1. Measure the caster sugar and keep it at the ready. Suspend
your large piping bag, nozzle down, in / over a large jug, so
that the wide cloth end is pulled back over the edge of the jug
for easy filling. Alternatively, using a large metal spoon to
sculpt the nests will give an attractive dune-like effect, so get
your metal spoon at the ready.

2. Preheat your oven(s). (If you have two ovens preheat one
to 180°C / 350°F / Gas Mark 4 and the other to 140°C / 275°F /
Gas Mark 1 – go for the higher temperature if you only have
one oven as this covers the first cooking stage).

3. Separate the eggs and whisk the egg whites in a large bowl.
As air bubbles begin to appear, add the salt and continue
whisking until smooth, stiff, white peaks are formed.
*Remember what is going on: the proteins are being unravelled and
coagulating with other de-natured proteins to form a film that holds*

in air bubbles; it is as if you are blowing up billions of balloons and creating them at the same time... Before the bubbles begin to collapse, immediately whisk in the sugar, half at a time. Add the cinnamon. Continue whisking until the sugar is evenly distributed and the meringue is smooth and peaky.

4. Fill the piping bag two-thirds full and begin by piping the base with a spiral of connecting meringue about 1 cm / ½ inch thick. Build up a shallow 4-cm / 1½-inch wall at the edge to contain the filling. Make the base of the wall thicker inside with an extra ring of meringue. Alternatively, sculpt a nest using a large metal spoon to make a flattish base with rounded walls. In both cases, the walls will need to be wedge shaped (thicker at the base) so they don't flop over in the oven.

5. Bake for 5–10 minutes to set the shell and prevent spreading. After this time, or as soon as any caramel colour appears, move immediately into the other oven or reduce the temperature to 140°C / 275°F / Gas Mark 1 for a further 1½–2 hours. It is important not to leave the meringue in the hot oven for too long as it will begin to puff up and lose its shape. When ready the Pavlova will be stiff with pleasantly cappuccino peaks. The inside should still be slightly gooey – test with a knife or lift gently to inspect the base. Remove from the oven and leave to cool. (When completely cold, the meringue can be stored in an airtight tin for at least a week).

6. Prepare your filling. If using *fresh fruit* avoid washing if at all possible. If necessary, quickly rinse in cold water and spread

out on a clean tea towel to dry, dabbing with kitchen paper. If including strawberries, remove the hulls. Set aside a few of the most perfect fruit to decorate the top, then cut the rest into pieces and combine with the rest of the fruit.

7. If using *frozen fruit*, spread the fruit out to defrost for at least an hour before needed, then transfer the fruit to a bowl with a slotted spoon, so you can collect any juices from the tray. Make up the volume of liquid to the required amount with apple juice, orange juice or water and 1 tablespoon sugar or agave. Mix the arrowroot with a little of the cold liquid in a pan until it has dissolved, then add the remaining liquid and gently bring to a simmer stirring constantly until thickened. Gently stir in the fruit and leave to cool.

8. As meringue desserts do not keep well once they are made, leave the final preparations until just before serving (they can be assembled 2 hours in advance, but not the day before).

9. Gently whip the cream until soft, glossy peaks that will hold their shape are formed. Stir in the sugar, if using, and spoon one third of the cream onto the base of the Pavlova, making a 5 mm–1 cm/¼–½ inch thick layer. Spoon the fruit over the cream, then cover with the remaining cream. Flute the cream up into peaks or pattern with a fork if you prefer. If you've used fresh fruit, decorate with a few fresh pieces. If you've used frozen, decorate with mint leaves, chocolate shavings or toasted flaked almonds. Edible flowers can also adorn your Pavlova just before serving.

CONJURING WITH FLAVOUR

◆

'The whole is bigger than the sum of its parts' is an old and familiar adage, oft quoted by holistic-science students and teachers alike. But it also has a resonance in our college kitchen, where we are forever conjuring with the magic of flavour.

SOMETIMES, WHEN YOU COMBINE INGREDIENTS, flavours arise that you would never have imagined to exist, and an unexpected taste sensation is created. Usually I can tell what will 'go with' another ingredient, but less familiar ingredients can bring surprise results. At other times, an unusual combination of familiar ingredients may bring out aspects of those ingredients that I hadn't previously noticed.

It's the same with people, and plants. Different situations – different 'companions' – can either detract from or enhance a relationship, by bringing out different qualities; and the way a relationship is handled is important, too. If you add cold milk to a hot soup and boil it, it will curdle. Likewise, throwing a newcomer into a job with an old hand on a very tight time schedule could literally 'sour' the relationship. With all these variables in the melting pot of cooking, and in life generally, the lesson is not to judge a situation until you have had the opportunity to appreciate fully what it means. And until you have given the ingredients (people, plants, relationships) the opportunity to prove themselves.

SORREL & SOUR-CREAM QUICHE

One beautiful example of the magic of flavour is the combination of lemony sorrel, sour cream, cheese and eggs, baked to scintillating perfection in a kind of savoury cheesecake.

It's only in the last ten years that I have come across sorrel as a cooking ingredient (apart from the tiny variety that grows in woods, which also has a lemony flavour, but is more food for mice than men). I should not have been surprised by the intense flavour, as the word 'sorrel' derives from the word 'sour', but I was. I was also stymied by the way the leaves behave when you cook them. Sorrel doesn't just cook down, like a sour version of spinach, but transforms into an almost gelatinous pulp, as soon as you cook it. Once combined with cheese, the flavour is so uniquely pleasant that it needs to be tasted to be imagined.

Serves *8–10*

Preparation time 1¼ hours, plus 20 minutes chilling

Baking time 40–50 minutes

Special equipment 28-cm/11-inch loose-based flan tin, lightly oiled

Ingredients

PASTRY

• Oil, for oiling • 1 quantity shortcrust pastry (see Spinach & Feta Lattice Tart on page 59, substituting 50 g/2 oz white flour with the same amount of brown or rye flour)

FILLING

• 1 large onion • 4 garlic cloves, chopped or 10 wild garlic
leaves • 2 tbsp olive oil • 300–500 g/10½–1 lb 2 oz French
sorrel leaves • Pinch of salt • Pinch of freshly ground black
pepper • 2–3 tbsp finely chopped fresh flat-leaf parsley
• 5 eggs • 300 ml/10 fl oz sour cream • 150 g/5 oz mature
Cheddar cheese • 25 g/1 oz grated Parmesan-like hard
cheese • 100 ml/4 fl oz milk • 1–2 tsp Dijon mustard

Method

1. Prepare your pastry following the instructions on page 60.
After chilling briefly, roll the pastry out on a floured surface
until it is about 3–4 mm (⅛ inch) thick. Roll up loosely on
your rolling pin, then lightly unroll over your prepared flan
tin. Press well into the corners, so no corner gaps are left,
then trim the pastry 5 mm/¼ inch above the top of the tin.
Flute the edge with your fingertips. Chill until needed.

2. Dice the onion. Crush or very finely chop the garlic, if
using. Alternatively, rough chop the wild garlic. Sauté the
onion and crushed garlic in the olive oil.

3. Rinse the sorrel, remove the stalks and shred the leaves
into narrow ribbons with a sharp knife. Add the sorrel (and
wild garlic if using) to the onions and cook briefly until
wilted. *Watch it turn olive green!* Leave to cool. Season minimally with pepper and salt. Stir in the chopped parsley.

4. Preheat your oven to 190°C/375°F/Gas Mark 5.

5. Combine the eggs, mustard, sour cream and milk. Whisk these together until a homogenous 'custardy' consistency is obtained.

6. Mix the sautéed sorrel and onion into the 'custard'. Stir in three quarters of the cheese, then tip into the pastry case and bake for 30 minutes. Sprinkle the remaining cheese on top and return to the oven for a further 10–20 minutes. If your oven has more heat at the bottom, make sure your quiche spends at least the first 20 minutes close to the bottom so the bases get well cooked (I find this all-in-one cooking method works better for quiches than blind baking the pastry case first – and avoids the problem of the pastry walls sinking).

7. Leave the quiche to stand for a couple of minutes, before removing the edges of the flan tin and serving.

VARIATION As the sorrel season coincides with the asparagus season, a lovely addition is to lay pre-cooked asparagus stems on top of the sorrel tart before cooking. Brush the asparagus with olive oil to prevent it drying out then sprinkle the extra cheese over the asparagus towards the end of cooking.

Beauty is Transient

People often say that my special-occasion cakes are 'a work of art' and ask me how I can bear it when they vanish so quickly. The truth is that I love the way 'edible art' disappears. For

many years I potted, painted and sewed; I took huge trouble to create permanent objects of beauty, but there was no guarantee they would find new owners – or even cupboard space!

When I make beautiful cakes I still spend time over them, putting goodness into every layer and adorning them. I still go into detail, sculpting marzipan mermaids or elephants – whatever is required. But I can truthfully say that I feel a sense of liberation when all is consumed and I can start baking my next creation. I love the transience of edible art. I think it has helped me get to grips with 'attachment', which, as I have mentioned, is one of the vices that becomes a focus of inner work on many people's spiritual journey.

The Perishability of Beauty

I once made marzipan models for a friend's wedding cake, and my friend was concerned about what to do with them afterwards. Would they dry out? Would they freeze? In the end, the heads got knocked off and they ended in the bin. Did I feel any attachment to them? Well, a little; I would rather they had been eaten! But I also felt guilty – I'd inadvertently transferred the problem of maintaining their beauty to my friend. Such pursuit of permanence often lures us into impossible places. I vowed to send out future cakes with a disclaimer: 'Close your eyes and consume quickly!'

YIN-YANG COOKIES

The dramatic swirling nature of these Yin-Yang Cookies – and the fact that they are quite complex to make – makes them perfect for an exercise in non-attachment and the transience of beauty. Making them will give you an opportunity to contemplate the truth of interconnectedness, as you cut out and reconnect the dark and light paisley teardrops of the Yin-and-Yang symbols, exchanging the centre of one for the centre of the other (see box).

Yin & Yang

In Chinese philosophy, images were used as a means of showing the underlying pattern of cosmic balance. Their purpose was not aesthetic, it was instructive, like a diagram. The concept of Yin and Yang represents the interconnected and interdependent nature of two seemingly contrary energies. Held together in a circle that represents 'everything', Yin is represented in the symbol by the black side with the white dot, Yang by the white side with the black dot. Yin is the dark, receptive, feminine side of things, as embodied by water; Yang is the bright, active, masculine side, as embodied by fire. Each contains an element of the other and cannot exist without the other. There is perpetual movement between the two, through which the harmony of the universe is maintained and everything within it is influenced.

MAKING THE CUTTER

As far as I know, a Yin-and-Yang cutter has not yet appeared in any shop, so I've made my own out of salt dough. This works well, but avoid getting it wet, or it will revert to dough! The jumbo size of the cookies has been dictated largely by the use of a common household item: the loo roll! The cutter should be made a day or two before you want to make the cookies as it will need to bake slowly and harden.

Preparation time 40–60 minutes

Baking time 4 hours

Ingredients & equipment

• 6 level tbsp plain white flour • 3 level tbsp fine salt • 2½ tbsp water • Baking parchment, including a piece about 15-cm /6-inch square • 2 loo rolls • Pencil • Compass • 4 paperclips • Vegetable oil • 1 baking tray • Sandpaper • 1 used marker pen

Method

1. Preheat your oven to 120°C/250°F/Gas Mark 1. Mix the flour, salt and water together in a bowl, then knead into a fairly stiff, pliable dough, that won't sag.

2. Fold the square of parchment in four to find the centre (and divide into four). Unfold. Make a dot in the middle, spread it out on the tray and place the loo rolls on either side of the centre point, with a dividing fold going straight through the middle of both. Move them so they are 5 mm/¼ inch

117

apart. This represents the thickness you will roll the dough out to. Mark the outside edge of the loo rolls, to give you the diameter of your cutter. Remove them and use a compass to draw a circle that connects the 2 outside dots.

3. Roll out the salt dough and cut into 2 x 2.5-cm/1-inch wide strips, about 5 mm/¼ inch thick at the most and each about 26 cm/10 inches long. Wrap baking parchment around the loo rolls to make them non-stick. Fasten with paperclips.

4. Thread the first strip in an 'S' shape around and between the 2 loo rolls so it wraps around half the base of each roll. Continue forming the shape of the symbol by curving the dough strip around the outside circle, keeping it as upright as possible and joining it together in three places with the other strip using a little water and a few smoothing pinches.

5. Bake your cutter for about 4 hours, removing the loo rolls half way through. When ready, the cutter will be hard and sound hollow when tapped. Leave to cool. If the cutter is not evenly dried out, return to the oven and bake a little more. File the cool, dry cutter with sandpaper to smooth and make sure the cutting edges are not too thick, then rub with oil.

6. *Care of your cutter:* never wash it in water. Wipe dry. If dropped in water, dry and re-harden in a low oven, if needed.

7. To make the round cutter for the centre of the teardrops, remove the barrel from an old marker pen and cut this with a bread knife so you have a 1 cm/½ inch deep ring of plastic, about 15–18 mm/¾ inch wide.

MAKING THE COOKIES

Makes *12 cookies*

Preparation time 1 hour

Baking time 20–30 minutes

Special equipment 1 baking tray, lined with baking parchment; 2-part home-made cookie cutter (*see pages 117–18*)

Ingredients

CHOCOLATE COOKIE DOUGH

• 40 g/1¼ oz rice flour • 140 g/5 oz plain white flour, plus extra for dusting • 85 g/3 oz muscovado sugar • Pinch of salt • 30 g/1 oz cocoa powder • 125 g/4½ oz butter • 1 egg yolk • 1 tsp light tahini

VANILLA COOKIE DOUGH

• 40 g/1¼ oz rice flour • 180 g/6½ oz plain white flour • 85 g/3 oz golden caster sugar • Pinch of fine salt • 125 g/4½ oz butter • 1 tsp light tahini • 1 egg yolk • ½ tsp vanilla extract

Method

1. Put the flour, sugar, salt, cocoa and butter for the chocolate dough into a bowl, then put the dry ingredients and butter for the vanilla dough into another bowl. Rub in the butter. I normally start with the vanilla mix then move on to the chocolate. Preheat your oven to 180°C/350°F/Gas Mark 4.

2. Once a breadcrumb consistency has formed, add the egg yolk and tahini. Add the vanilla extract to the plain mixture, mix well , then press into two fairly soft, malleable doughs.

3. On a clean lightly floured surface or tray, roll out half the vanilla dough to about 7 mm / ¼ inch thick. Roll out half the chocolate dough similarly. Make sure they don't stick.

4. Use your cutter to cut through or press in an impression into the dough. Finish the cutting with a knife if necessary (this is a fairly clumsy cutter as cutters go!).

5. Arrange your yin yang cookies on the baking tray, *uniting the positive yin with the negative yang.* Cut out the middle of the teardrop with your plastic cutter and build up a stack of chocolate yins, vanilla yangs, before inserting these contrasting coloured dots in each cookie. *This exchange reminds us that everything must contain a little of its opposite for there to be balance and a pathway for the perpetual movement that makes up our universe. This is the secret of interdependence.* Use your fingers to gently press the pieces together, so they form a round disk. (They will fuse together in the oven.) Bake for about 20–30 minutes until the vanilla outer edges are beginning to turn golden brown. When ready, leave to cool on the baking tray for a minute or two before carefully transferring to a wire rack. Once cold, store in an airtight tin.

VARIATION Make Swirl Cookies by rolling out two dough rectangles, put one on top of the other and roll them together into logs. Refrigerate then slice off 5 mm / ¼ inch wide swirls.

FOOD OF THE GODS

◆

The Aztecs attributed the creation of the cocoa plant to their god of intelligence and self-reflection, Quetzalcóatl. Descending from heaven on the beam of a morning star, he carried with him a cocoa tree that had been stolen from paradise. It was the first of many plants he would cultivate with people, as (now in human form) he instilled new knowledge and brought a civilizing influence.

WHAT IS IT THAT MAKES CHOCOLATE so irresistibly delicious? Could it be to do with its chemistry? Chocolate is rich in phenylethylamine (PEA), which occurs naturally in the brain and is associated with the euphoric feelings of falling in love. Furthermore its mother plant, the cacao tree, was named *Theobroma Cacao* by Linnaeus – meaning 'food of the gods' – and had great ceremonial importance for the Aztecs and Maya people, who used the beans as currency, and mixed them with chilli and other spices before offering them to the gods and using them to anoint newborn babies.

The journey of cacao to Europe has been attributed to Hernando Cortés, who conquered part of Mexico in 1519. Cortés realized that the beans had both financial and gourmet potential. Not only did he establish cocoa plantations, but he presented beans to the Spanish king, Charles V, along with the means of turning them into a drink. Although chocolate has now spread worldwide, it is still regarded as a treat.

Beware the Dietary Demon!

But is it 'treat' enough? Chocolate (especially the dark variety) contains valuable nutritional properties: minerals, as well as vitamins and antioxidants that can help keep blood pressure down; and PEA, which can act as a slight antidepressant by increasing levels in the brain of the neurotransmitter known as serotonin. However, chocolate is far from being a wonder-drug, and only a small quantity of dark chocolate needs to be eaten to benefit from its properties. The problem is that chocolate also contains varying amounts of sugar – a dietary demon that needs to be kept strictly under wraps.

The danger of our diet being linked to vested interests (in either business or political terms) is enormous and has had severe repercussions on our health. In *Fat Chance: The Hidden Truth about Sugar, Obesity and Disease,* paediatrician and author Dr Robert H. Lustig reveals how research into the effect of the high-carb diet that went hand-in-hand with the low-fat diet promoted in the Seventies and Eighties has shown that obesity levels increased, because the different good and bad forms of cholesterol had not been properly identified. The consumption of high-fructose corn syrup that made low-fat foods palatable enabled bad forms of cholesterol to slip through the net, switched off our natural appetite-suppressing hormone (leptin) and led to an increase in 'metabolic-syndrome' diseases, such as obesity and Type 2 diabetes. Carbs in the form of high-fructose corn syrup present in soft drinks

are one of the deadliest perpetrators of the dietary imbalance. Since its introduction in 1975 it has found its way into millions of products, contributing to the 64 kg / 141 lb of sugar consumed each year by the average American.

There has been much publicity about the danger of eating fructose independent of the fibre that naturally accompanies it and helps to trigger an appropriate sense of fullness in relation to the volume of sweetness consumed. Some books advocate eliminating anything sweet from your diet, while other practitioners try to restore a sense of balance and to educate for awareness.

For example, based at ucsf's Division of Endocrinology and Metabolism, Dr Lustig introduced a code to the young people he worked with, which involved not only getting rid of all sugared liquid, but always eating carbs with fibre, waiting for second helpings, and taking regular exercise to balance sedentary 'screen-time'. This formula works for reasons that may challenge the notion of calories that we've grown up with. Physical exercise is part of the equation not only because it's a way to burn calories but because it is also a stress- and appetite-reducer and leads to improved insulin sensitivity.

A Dangerous Dose

Recent literature that describes sugar as a 'poison' is quite scary and cannot be ignored by any cook. Dr Lustig's book *Fat Chance* is one such example, as is David Gillespie's *Sweet Poison:*

Chocolate Meditation

Chocolate-eating is sometimes used as a popular exercise for practising mindful awareness. You can unwrap your bar of chocolate slowly, smell it, break off a chunk and let it melt on your tongue. Notice how the texture changes as it slowly melts, and reflect on the different flavour notes that come through. You can also turn this exercise upside-down and make it into a meditation in *non*-attachment, accompanying the same actions with the mantra 'I am enjoying this bar of chocolate knowing these flavours will pass, just as the scent of roses in summer diminishes and loving them I let them go.'

Why Sugar Makes Us Fat. Meanwhile, Dr Mark Hyman, founder of the Ultra Wellness Centre in Massachusetts and author of the *Blood Sugar Solution 10-Day Detox Diet*, has called sugar 'more addictive than cocaine and nicotine' sparking off press headlines that describe sugar as 'the new tobacco'. But, as Dr David Katz, medical director for the Integrative Medicine Centre in Connecticut, commented recently, 'It's not sugar that's the poison, but the dose that makes the poison.'[1] It comes back to us adults to educate ourselves, and be mindful of what we're eating and feeding others. We need to become the purveyors of balance and endeavour to teach the same to our children.

---

[1] 'Sugar *Isn't* Evil: A Rebuttal' by Dr David Katz, *The Huffington Post*, 18 April 2011 (accessed on www.huffingtonpost.com, June 2014)

At Schumacher College, we serve dessert just once a week – plus a cake, if it is someone's birthday. Observing this, a friend of mine, Wendy Cook, reminded me on many occasions that it was important not to deprive ourselves of that occasional touch of heaven! To support this she mentioned Rudolf Steiner's observation that children who were deprived of sweetness would be found 'pilfering' – they would be missing a necessary connection not just with sweetness, but with 'heaven'. It is this advice that I often think of when the question of sugar comes up, and it reminds me of the role home cooks have as providers of healthy sweet treats – ones that are not laced with fructose corn syrup and other additives. The following chocolate cake recipes cater for two extremes of indulgence. The first can be created in an over-the-top gateau style. The second embraces the wisdom of combining fibre with sweetness, in a cake that's (almost) sugar-free.

SPECKLED CHOCOLATE & RASPBERRY GATEAU

This is a Victoria sandwichy-type cake that can be dressed up or down, depending on the occasion and the season. I first made it on a whim when a visitor was coming to tea and I had some leftover chocolate icing. I decided to experiment by grating and folding it into a spongy-golden cake mix. The grated curls were so abundant that I kept some to sprinkle on top. Later, I baked again, adding cream and raspberries, so choose your own level of extravagance.

Makes *1 small gateau, serving 8*

Preparation time 1 hour, plus 2 hours chilling

Baking time 20–25 minutes

Special equipment 2 x 18-cm/7-inch round sandwich tins, greased with butter and lined with baking parchment

Ingredients

CHOCOLATE 'CHEESE' – FOR GRATING

• 100 g/3½ oz plain chocolate, at least 70% cocoa solids
• 40 g/1½ oz butter

CAKE

• 85 g/3 oz butter, softened, plus extra for greasing
• 125 g/4½ oz golden granulated sugar • Grated zest of ½ organic orange • Juice of 1 small orange • ½ tsp vanilla extract • 3 eggs, separated • 125 g/4½ oz plain or self-raising white flour • 50 g/2 oz ground almonds • Pinch of salt
• 2¼ tsp baking powder (if using plain flour)

FILLING

• 4 tbsp raspberry jam • 140 ml/5 fl oz whipping or double cream • 100 g/3–4 oz fresh raspberries (optional)

ICING (THIS GOES UNDER THE CURLS!)

• 50 g/2 oz plain chocolate • 25 g/1 oz butter
• 1 tbsp orange juice or water

Method

1. Make the 'chocolate cheese' by melting the chocolate and butter together in a heatproof bowl set over a pan of barely simmering water. As it melts, stir until smooth. Cool for a few minutes then pour into an old margarine tub (or similar small container). Chill to set for 2 hours, or overnight.

2. Turn out and grate the set 'choc-cheese' on the coarse side of your grater, holding it with a plastic bag. Reserve one third of the curliest and most perfect chocolate shavings. Keep all the curls in plastic boxes in the fridge until ready to use.

3. Preheat your oven to 180°C/350°F/Gas Mark 4.

4. Cream the butter and sugar together in a bowl, then add the zest, juice and vanilla, followed by the egg yolks.

5. Mix the flour, ground almonds, salt and baking powder, if using, together in another bowl and set aside.

6. In another bowl, whisk the egg whites into snowy peaks, then fold the dry ingredients into the creamed butter mixture in two or three batches. Give the egg whites a few extra whisks to return them to the height of their foamy glory, then genty fold in half of them to loosen the mixture then gently fold in the rest. Finally, fold in the reserved two thirds of the chocolate curls, but don't mix too much.

7. Spoon the cake mixture into your prepared tins and bake for 20–25 minutes. The cake is ready when it's well risen, golden brown and set to touch – a skewer inserted in the middle will come out clean but moist. Leave to stand for a

few minutes then go around the edge of the tin with a knife. Turn out onto a plate and then invert back on to a wire rack to finish cooling (if you tip it straight out onto the wire rack its top will get squashed down).

8. Find a plate that holds the cake in position well, ideally with the rounded top down and the base up (so no cake has to be carved off). Spread the jam over the uppermost side, then spread a layer of whipped cream on top. It should be spread in a thick layer *almost* to the edge. Press raspberries into the cream if you want to go for the fancier option. Place the top of the cake on the cream and gently push down, very slightly, so a tempting bulge of cream is visible.

9. To adorn the cake with luscious curls of chocolate, prepare your 'glue' by making the icing. Gently melt the chocolate, butter and orange juice or water in a heatproof bowl set over a pan of barely simmering water. Don't be tempted to stir until you notice about half the chocoloate beginning to melt; then, stir smooth. Next, use a knife to spread it in a thin layer over the top of the cake, encouraging the icing to dribble tantalizingly over the edges. Leave to cool a little – test its temperature by dropping one curl on at a time to check it's not going to melt. If it does, wait a bit longer. When ready, sprinkle the curls on the top from the box. The icing will hold the curls in place as it sets. Alternatively, deck with more whipped cream (double the quantities given) and toss the curls over this, gateaux-style.

DATE, CHOCOLATE & ALMOND CAKE

This moist, truly delicious and almost sugar-free chocolate cake relies on dates for its sweetness. Dates have been eagerly traded for centuries, long before the spread of cane sugar. They were popular with the Romans, and desert Arabs often lived on them for long periods of time, combining them only with milk.

Not surprisingly, the main food value of dates lies in their high (50–70 per cent) sugar content, which makes them great for replenishing energy; and, unlike conventional refined sucrose, these simple sugars are combined with a fair amount of protein, valuable minerals (not unlike those found in chocolate) and vitamins A, B and K. Importantly, dates are also rich in dietary fibre that prevents LDL (the bad kind of cholesterol) being absorbed in the gut.

This recipe is wheat- and gluten-free, with ground almonds and polenta being added instead of flour. Because the dark chocolate in the recipe contains some sugar, this cake isn't truly sugar-free. However, if you substitute the chocolate with cocoa and cocoa butter (melting the latter in the same way as chocolate), you'll get a truly sucrose-free cake that is a bit less sweet and slightly more expensive!

Makes *1 medium-sized cake; 10–12 slices*

Preparation time 45 minutes, plus 1 hour soaking

Baking time 30–40 minutes

Special equipment 22-cm/8½-inch round cake tin, greased with butter and lined with baking parchment

Ingredients

• 85 g / 3 oz butter, plus extra for greasing • 175 g / 6 oz stoned dates • 2 oranges • 2 tbsp honey • 150 g / 5 ½ oz plain chocolate, at least 70% cocoa solids (or use 50 g / 2 oz cocoa powder and 50 g / 2 oz cocoa butter / creamed coconut for a completely sugar-free version) • 2 eggs • 50 g / 2 oz ground almonds • 25 g / 1 oz polenta • ½ tsp ground cinnamon • Pinch of salt • 1 tsp baking powder

ICING

• 85 g / 3 oz plain chocolate, at least 70% cocoa solids or 25 g / 1 oz cocoa powder and 50 g / 2 oz cocoa butter / creamed coconut for a completely sugar-free version • 1 rounded tbsp (15 g / ½ oz) butter • 1 tsp honey • 1 tbsp sour cream or double cream

DECORATION

• 15–20 whole almonds • 5–6 stoned dates

Method

1. Chop the dates into small pieces and put them in a bowl. Grate the outermost zest from the oranges and add to the dates, then squeeze the juice and mix this in too. Leave the dates to soak for an hour before cooking gently in a saucepan until the dates soften. Keep stirring to prevent them burning, adding a little more orange juice if necessary. The dates should

mush up into a fairly thick purée. Break up the lumps with your spoon or blend the mixture if you want it completely smooth. Stir in the honey and tip into a large bowl.

2. Chop and gently melt the chocolate and butter in a heat-proof bowl set over a saucepan of barely simmering water.

3. Preheat your oven to 180°C/350°F/Gas Mark 4.

4. Add the eggs to the (now cooler) date mixture.

5. Mix the ground almonds, polenta, cinnamon, salt and baking powder in a bowl. Add the chocolate mixture to the date/egg mixture, then fold in the dry ingredients; mix well.

6. Tip the batter into the prepared cake tin and bake for 30–40 minutes. When ready, the cake should feel fairly firm to touch and a skewer inserted in the middle should come out clean. Leave to cool in the tin for 20 minutes before turning carefully out onto a wire rack.

7. For the decoration, preheat the oven to 200°C/400F/Gas Mark 6. If using almonds with skins on, 'blanch' by immersing in boiling water for 2 minutes, then draining and slipping off the skins. Spread the nuts out on a baking tray and roast them for about 10 minutes until light brown in colour. Leave to cool. Slice across the dates into rings, or lengthways for ovals.

8. When the cake is cool, make the icing. Chop the chocolate and melt gently with the butter and honey in a double boiler. Remove from the heat and stir in the sour cream or cream.

9. Spread the icing on the top and around the edges. Swirl the top with a fork and decorate with the almonds and dates.

FOOD FOR FRIENDS

The longer days bring with them warmer weather and the enticement to get up a little earlier and do more outside. Every year spring surprises me — it is scintillating and brings reassurance that continuity and renewal go hand-in-hand. First the spring flowers: snowdrops, crocuses, daffodils, primroses; then the leafy green shoots, wild garlic, nettle — all filled with vital energies that we cooks can tap into as we conjure up nurturing foods for others.

SPRING IN OUR STEP

This year there seems to be a spring in our Devon community, too. It is a cultural revival that is moving from dreams to reality, putting out runners and planting new roots like a strawberry plant. For me, it is like the coming of spring.

WHEN I FIRST CAME TO LIVE IN TOTNES there were several bakeries on the high street that sold bread, buns and cakes. I used to go to them for fresh yeast. After about ten years three of them closed down, leaving just one that baked its own bread. Owners retired, no one wanted to buy the businesses, and the baking machinery was sold off. More clothes shops came to the high street and more shops filled with upmarket bric-a-brac.

Elsewhere in the world, however, the nascent artisan bread movement was already taking hold, with Real Bread bakeries in America well ahead of those in the UK. In Europe, the artisan style of sourdough bread-making remains a source for reinvigorating our own baking, despite the fact that in France the 'baguette culture' has halved since the Seventies, to just half a baguette per person per day – whereas 100 years ago it was three baguettes a day. Germany, by contrast, can boast the highest per capita consumption of bread worldwide, which may be a testament to its healthy traditions of whole-wheat and rye sourdough-making.

The Transition Movement

A decade later, the HQ of the Transition movement, which seeks less energy-hungry ways of living, in an era of change, has rooted itself in Totnes High Street, attracting interest from visitors all over the world. When an idea is right for its time, it seems that it can spread like wildfire, sowing itself in the fertile territories of our minds and catching the imagination everywhere. Building 'community resilience', as we proceed to an oil-free and more sustainable future, is the key to Transition and finds many forms of expression, from working on a psychological level to practical action, as well as schemes that emphasize community building and skill-shares.

The redevelopment of a local food system is central to reducing our dependency on imported produce, as well as reducing our carbon footprint. Holly Tiffen is a committed localist or even 'locavore' (an American phrase!) who has been charged with the task of running the 'Food Links' arm of Transition Town Totnes (TTT): getting together local suppliers and producers to create food hubs, and looking at what is needed to harness community resources, in terms of produce, people-power and processing facilities. As a result, many pop-up restaurants and skill-shares have appeared, and a community kitchen has been born in Totnes town hall. At a (literally) grass-roots level, Food Links is now embarking on a project to get farmers planting more oats, because they do well in this damp part of Devon.

Meanwhile in Birmingham, Britain's second-largest city, Real Bread aficionado Tom Baker opened the Loaf shop and cookery school as a social enterprise. Formerly an NHS nutritionist, Tom is passionate about promoting real food and healthy living in Birmingham and in building community through food: 'This means bringing back forgotten food skills and real food to our kitchens through our cookery courses, community baking and pop-up events and helping restore the local High Street at the same time.'[1]

The Real Bread Movement at Home
Official government statistics suggest that the decline of Totnes' high-street bakeries in the late Nineties was part of a general national decline. The number of businesses involved in the manufacture of bread, pastry goods and cakes decreased from 2,226 in 1997 to 1,603 in 2006. However, by 2010 almost 300 more such businesses were listed (1,892 in total). On the Real Bread Campaign's very useful 'Real Bread Finder' search facility, 600 'Real Bread' bakeries are listed, while the National Association of Master Bakers' statistics state that there are 4,500 small craft bakeries in the UK. The Flour Advisory Bureau suggests that 13 per cent of British adults bake bread at home. All this should mean that pure, healthy bread without additives is being consumed by more and more people, whether it is made at home or bought in a small bakery. As a percentage of the estimated 12 million loaves

---

[1] 'About Us', Loafonline.co.uk, accessed June 2014

sold each day in the UK, this is still a drop in the ocean, but it's heading in the right direction and gives enormous hope.

In 2011 the Real Bread Campaign launched *Knead to Know*, the introductory guide to success in bringing Real Bread to the heart of your local community. For anyone wanting to set up a bakery, this book gives good practical advice and encouragement; a survey in March 2012 showed that 22 per cent of those who had read it had gone on to set up bakeries, and 39 per cent were planning to do so.[1] If, however, what you want is to improve your own bread-making skills, the Real Bread Campaign's website is a good place to begin your search for a teacher. Its ambassadors are some of the finest teachers including: Aidan Chapman, Master Baker and founder of the Phoenix Bakery, who teaches bread-baking at Hugh Fearnley Whittingstall's River Cottage Cookery School; Richard Bertinet of the Bertinet Kitchen in Bath; and Emmanuel Hadjiandreou of the School of Artisan Food. They have produced books (*see pages 140–41*) that will take you further into baking than we have journeyed in our pursuit of mindfulness (though you can take mindfulness with you, as you travel through any cookbook).

The Real Bread Movement Abroad

In the USA and Australia the same pattern of baker-turned-teacher is also to be found. Dan Leader runs the huge artisan Bread Alone Bakery in New York City, and teaches at the Institute of Culinary Education in New York City. Travelling

[1] Real Bread Campaign, realbreadcampaign.org (http://www.sustainweb.org/real-bread/facts_figures/, accessed June 2014)

to Europe to garner bread-making tips for his recent book, *Local Breads*, Dan describes how much more attentive to the wheat quality European bakers are, and how gentle they are in their milling.

Not far from the Bread Alone Bakery is another artisan set-up: the Sullivan Street Bakery. Here, almost a decade ago, Jim Lahey pioneered a no-knead method of baking artisan-style loaves, using a pot that goes in the oven. The technique has influenced home bakers, and we frequently use this method at the College to produce huge, well-aerated loaves.

Just as in the UK, where a community, for sharing artisan bread-making ideas has evolved around the Real Bread Campaign, the strong artisan community of people who really care about bread continues to evolve in the USA. This has been developing for some 30 years, since Dan Leader founded Bread Alone and Steve Sullivan founded the Acme Bakery Company in San Francisco, and is sustained by young bakers such as Chad Robertson of the Tartine Bakery in San Francisco. So impressed was author Michael Pollan by Chad's approach that he apprenticed himself to Chad while writing the book *Cooked*. 'Chad's just so thoughtful about what he's doing... Every loaf of bread matters' said Pollan.[1]

Hearth, Home & Companionship

This brings us neatly back to the hearth: its fire and its hot stones – its perfect formula for baking. Oh, how I love it

[1] 'Rising Star: Chad Robertson of San Francisco's Tartine Bakery and Café' by Oliver Strand, *Vogue,* July 2013

when my bread rises another inch in the oven, and I know I've put it in at exactly the right moment to get it maximally risen. And the joy when my cakes don't sink in the middle!

As mentioned earlier (*see page 53*), you may want to buy a stone (or ceramic insert) to make your oven more like a brick oven – and more like Hestia's hearth! For many breadbakers, this heavy piece of equipment is absolutely critical to obtain the best success – and it can be left in your oven as a permanent fixture which may benefit the rest of your baking. When it comes to mindful baking, however, it is good just to know that this is a possibility, should you want to go further in the art of the hearth.

It's not just a deepening of awareness through the process of baking that brings mindfulness, but the sharing of what we bake. Sharing happens on many levels: at home and in the community; as a receiver and as a giver; with and without the exchange of money. When baking with awareness, we deepen our connection not only to our ingredients and our methods, but to our fellows. The word 'company' derives from the Latin *cum panis*, and means literally 'with bread'. In choosing our *companions* – or 'with bread ones' – to eat with, teach and learn from, we are sending out a big YES for continuity into the future: YES for our way of being, and for our real and wholesome values. And all this spirals out from the hearth, the warm heart of the home where there is a cosiness that nurtures friendship and the fire that bakes bread.

ORGANIZATIONS WORKING
TOWARDS POSITIVE CHANGE

Action for Happiness
www.actionforhappiness.org
A movement of people committed to building
a happier society

Baking a Smile
www.bakingasmile.org
A not-for-profit organization that makes cakes
for children with life-limiting conditions and
their siblings

Bread Matters, Scotland
www.breadmatters.com
Andrew Whitley offers baking courses, some
of which include the practical knowledge
needed to run a bakery

**Ethical Consumer Research
Association, Manchester**
www.ethicalconsumer.org
Helps you make ethical choices about
the food you buy; publishes the Ethical
Consumer magazine

Plum Village Centre, Dordogne, France
www.plumvillage.org
The spiritual community founded by
Vietnamese Zen monk Thich Nhat Hanh

Real Bread Campaign/Sustain, London
www.sustainweb.org/realbread
National organization championing
community artisan bakeries; helps you
search for Real Bread, and baking lessons,
in your area

Roots of Change, San Francisco
www.rootsofchange.org
Works to develop and support a sustainable
food system in California by 2030

Schumacher College, Devon
www.schumachercollege.org.uk
Offers postgraduate and short courses
that offer transformative learning for a
sustainable future

**Slow Food International,
Bra (Cuneo), Italy**
www.slowfood.com
Global grass-roots eco-gastronomic
organization that aims to protect good
food, its enjoyment, its community and
its environment from the homogenization
of globalization

Slow Food UK, London
www.slowfood.org.uk
Slow Food USA, New York
www.slowfoodusa.org

**Virtuous Bread &
Bread Angels, London**
www.virtuousbread.com
A social enterprise working around the UK
and beyond, running bread-making workshops
with community groups that are facing a wide
range of issues, and helping to set up home
micro-bakeries

BOOKS THAT TEACH,
INSPIRE & INFORM

Bread Alone: *Bold fresh loaves from your
own hands,* Daniel Leader & Judith Blahnik,
William Morrow, 1993

Bread Matters: *Why & how to make your own,*
Andrew Whitley, Fourth Estate, 2009

Changing Diets, Changing Minds:
How food affects mental health & behaviour,
Courtney Van de Weyer, Real Bread
Campaign/Sustain, 2005

Cooked: *A natural history of transformation,*
Michael Pollan, Allen Lane 2013

Crust: *Bread to get your teeth into,*
Richard Bertinet, Kyle Cathie, 2007

Fat Chance: *The hidden truth about sugar,
obesity & disease,* Dr Robert Lustig,
Fourth Estate, 2014

Flow: *The psychology of happiness,*
Mihaly Csikszentmihalyi, Rider, 2002

Gluten-Free and Vegan Bread: *Artisanal recipes to make at home,* Jennifer Katzinger, Sasquatch Books, 2012

The Handmade Loaf: *Contemporary European recipes for the home baker,* Dan Lepard, Mitchell Beazley, 2008

In Defence of Food: *The myth of nutrition and the pleasures of eating,* Michael Pollan, Penguin, 2009

Knead to Know: *The real bread starter,* Real Bread Campaign, 2011

Local Breads: *Sourdough and whole-grain recipes from Europe's best artisan bakers,* Daniel Leader with Lauren Chattman, W.W. Norton & Co., 2007

Mindfulness: *Be mindful, live in the moment,* Gill Hasson, Capstone, 2013

The Omnivore's Dilemma: *The search for a perfect meal in a fast-food world,* Michael Pollan, Bloomsbury, 2011

The Seasonal Detox Diet: *Remedies from the ancient cookfire,* Carrie L'Esperance, Healing Arts Press, 1998

Small is Beautiful: *A study of economics as if people mattered,* E.F. Schumacher, Abacus 1991

Tartine Bread, Chad Robertson, Chronicle Books, 2010

Tassajara Bread Book, Edward Espe Brown, Shambala, 1996

The Miracle of Mindfulness: *The classic guide to meditation by the world's most revered master,* Thich Nhat Hanh, Beacon Press, 1987; Rider, 2008

The Power of Now: *A guide to spiritual enlightenment,* Eckhart Tolle, Hodder, 2001

Rising Up: *Baking real bread improves people's lives,* Chris Young, Real Bread Campaign/ Sustain, 2013

Sweet Poison: *Why sugar makes us fat* David Gillespie, Penguin, 2008

The Bertinet Kitchen, Bath, UK
www.thebertinetkichen.com

Loaf Bakery & Cookery School, Birmingham, UK
www.loafonline.co.uk

River Cottage Cookery School, Devon, UK
www.rivercottage.net

The School of Artisan Food, Nottinghamshire, UK
www.schoolofartisanfood.org

International Culinary Center, New York, USA
www.internationalculinarycenter.com

San Francisco Baking Institute, USA
www.sfbi.com

Brasserie Bread, Melbourne & Sydney, Australia
www.brasseriebread.com.au

La Cuisine Paris, France
www.lacuisineparis.com

SUPPLIERS OF ORGANIC FLOUR (MAIL-ORDER AVAILABLE)

Doves Farm, Berkshire
www.dovesfarm.co.uk
Offers a wide range of flours, including gluten-free blends; informative online site

King Arthur Flour, Vermont, USA
www.kingarthurflour.com
Its Baker's Catalogue offers a wide choice of flours and baking equipment

Shipton Mill, Gloucestershire
www.shipton-mill.com
The online shop sells proving baskets and fresh yeast, as well as flours

Stoate & Sons, Dorset
www.stoatesflour.co.uk
Its range of organic flours includes locally milled grains

NOTEWORTHY ARTISAN BAKING SCHOOLS

INDEX

DEDICATION

*For my father, who was a very mindful cook and taught me
an important lesson while he was chopping parsley: even when you
know how do things quickly sometimes it is nicer to do things slowly,
just because you want to. (The reverse is also true!)*

ACKNOWLEDGEMENTS

*I would like to thank the wonderful team of editors at
Leaping Hare Press, especially Monica Perdoni, Jayne Ansell,
Mandy Greenfield and Kim Davies, for their unwavering enthusiasm
and support for this project, and Satish Kumar for his constant
encouragement. I would also like to thank Tara Vaughan-Hughes for
her insights into the bread-making scene in North America and
for sharing her bread-knotting skills with me, and Sarah Jackson for
letting me pick her brains about sourdough, particularly pain
Poilâne. I would also like to thank Andrew Whitley for his inspiration
and generous sharing of leaven and bread skills, and the Real Bread
Campaign for championing Real Bread in the UK and putting it
firmly back on the map for all to enjoy. And finally, thanks to my
husband Stephan Harding and my son Oscar for being my tasters.*